TANTRIC
SEX

TANTRIC
SEX

by
E.J. GOLD AND CYBELE GOLD

Illustrated by George Metzger

PEAK SKILL

PEAK SKILL TANTRIC LOVE SERIES

Sexual Energy Ecstasy
Tantric Sex

Copyright © 1978 by Lana C. Gold
Copyright © 1988 Additional Material by E.J. Dorfman
All Rights Reserved

Tantric Sex is a revised and expanded edition of material first published in 1978 by I.D.H.H.B., Inc. — Hohm Press under the title Beyond Sex.

First Peak Skill Edition 1988
First printing 1988
ISBN: 0-917879-02-3
Library of Congress Catalog Card Number: 88-2551

Library of Congress Cataloging in Publication Data

Gold, E. J.
    Tantric sex.

    1. Sex--Miscellanea. 2. Yoga. 3. Tantrism.
I. Gold, Cybele. II. Title.
BF1999.G6218 1988   133   88-2551
ISBN 0-917879-02-3 (pbk.)

Printed in the United States of America

PEAK SKILL PUBLISHING, P.O. Box 5489, Playa Del Rey, CA 90296

Cover design and lettering by Gerow Reece

Foreword

Tantric Sex is a practical guide to the theory and methods of sex yoga for the West by acknowledged spiritual authorities. Once the privileged possession of select initiates, the sexospiritual secrets revealed in this book are just the right remedy for an ailing society that suppresses the power that gave it life.

The material is presented in a straightforward, step-by-step format that facilitates performance. While just reading this book may inspire or encourage you, actually doing the exercises with a partner will certainly transform you. The power of sex yoga, especially when utilized with maximum spiritual efficiency as a form of intentional stress, can literally open the door to establishment in higher realms of consciousness. It is for this reason that the ancient texts prescribed Tantric sex only for the hero or heroine.

Like the ancient Sutras, the section "Journey Through The Great Mother" is highly condensed and designed for deep meditation. Offering practical instruction as well as being replete with striking imagery, it is perhaps a description of Kundalini awakening. Its emphasis on the Void is in welcome contrast to some contemporary "Tantric" teachings that promote bliss without insight. For some, the easiest way to appreciate these Sutras has been listening to the tape recorded version with musical accompaniment by E.J. Gold.

The Objective (Tantric) Sex experimental reports are taken from an actual workshop. These reports of personal experiences are but a few of the thousands of extraordinary experiences available via these techniques. After all, you create your experiences in Inner Space and you are, in truth, infinitely creative. As a practical note, follow the Debriefing Routine or a similar form of gradual re-entry when you return to BodySpace. Otherwise, a shock may ensue as it can be difficult to assess just how far out you have been.

The exercises are presented in stages from beginning to advanced levels. It is recommended that you include the beginning exercises however simple they may seem. They are quite powerful and will help you accomplish the deconditioning that is the prerequisite for success at Tantra. Again, it is by doing, and not by thinking about it, that results are achieved.

There is a great deal of concentrated material in this book, enough to occupy a lifetime. Also, the techniques can be combined with the meditation techniques of other traditions. For example, I have enjoyed blending Buddhist mindfulness practices with these methods.

So, take your time and feel free to experiment. Most importantly, do it with love for yourself and your partner.

The bliss, responsibilities and revelations of Tantric sex await you!

David Alan Ramsdale
Los Angeles
October, 1987

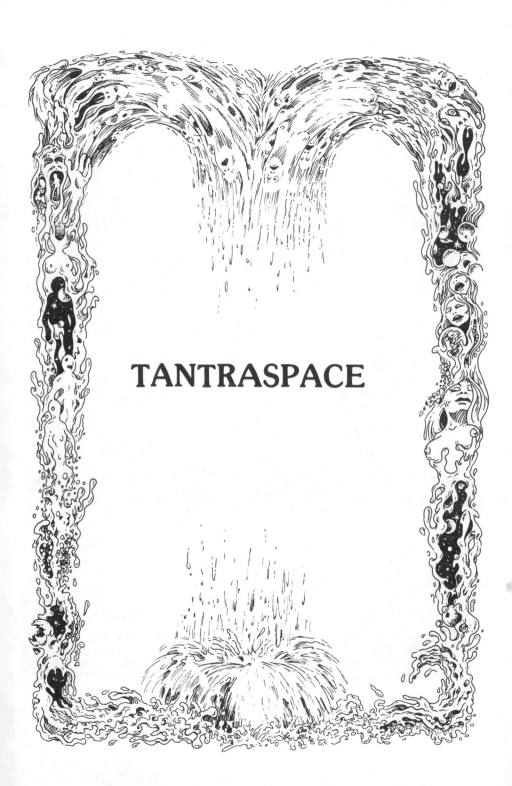

TANTRASPACE

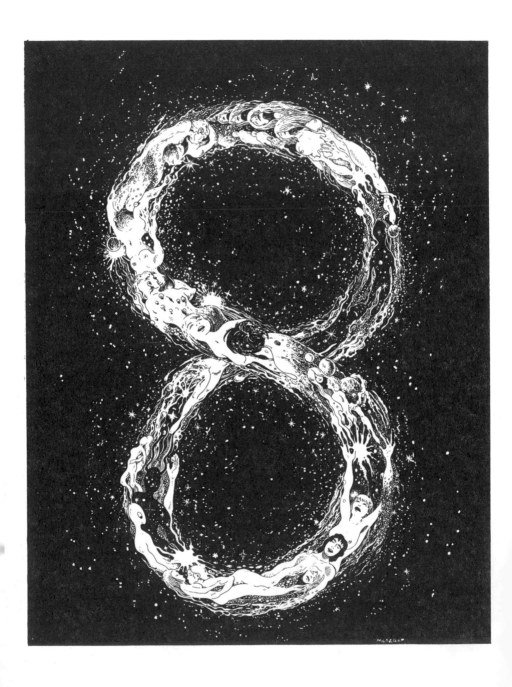

Tantraspace

Gently and slowly the couple begin their simultaneous deep breathing, which builds into a Silent Humming Mantra* as they visualize in each other the form of the Cosmic Couple. The room is semi-dark, and their eyes remain open.

They begin to manifest the reflected image of the universe, using the Sensing Exercise** to perceive their bodies united as a single entity. This creates an etheric tube which exists for a while, and then disappears into formlessness.

They sit up and firmly merge their foreheads together by gentle pressure. As they do this, they get a clear image of seeing themselves as they both form a *double body* . They continue this until neither one is aware of a separate identity.

They are now able to observe the double body from above and outside. They are without form, yet

*See page 67.
**See page 60.

sensing it through feelings. As they watch, stars begin to appear within the double body. They burn brightly, and do not pulse.

The couple remain motionless in this space as they transfer closer and closer to the absolute void. There is a feeling of willingness to share this experience fully; that everything which was done in existence belongs to existence. They have scaled above the world of action and reaction, cause and effect.

The feeling of the sourceness of one another is shared, and as their inner worlds merge, their mental and emotional viewpoints become one. They accept easily the great welling of sensation and perception which accompanies the expansion of being everywhere and nowhere.

A feeling of amused confusion and disorientation develops, combined with a euphoric disinterest in what is going to happen, if anything. They are in complete instantaneous communication without the need to verbalize or gesture.

A slow awareness builds in them that they were never on the Earth, but that instead they received impressions as if living in bodies because they could perceive sensations as if living in a body. Without those sensations, space and time would never have had any effect on them.

They find themselves reverting now to their natural state of being, from which they never actually departed except in dreams. They see now that Earth was only a co-created state of existence which required effort to keep it real, and that by ceasing this effort they automatically return to their native state.

They could make separate identities again if they wished to. Of course they know that they can always play that game again, and that they will sooner or later return to it. After all, what else have they to do with eternity?

They allow the feelings of "having been human" to subside in them. They have no idea where all this will lead them, but they accept what is happening, because this is the way it is.

They enjoy the swirling flow which takes their collective consciousness from one point to another within the formless void. A definite vibration is building, and they experience a strong sensation as if they are about to shake apart or explode. They approach a gateway of some kind, at which there is a guardian. They acknowledge his presence, and move through into another space on a higher level.

The distinction between their consciousness is rapidly disappearing. Soon it will be impossible for them to decide with which body they came into this. Their awareness is linked with a form somehow holding the world in its hands and yet at the same time flowing into it. They have drifted into identification with the Cosmic Couple.

A slow intermingling has begun, in which their former identities are so convoluted that consciousness breaks away and knowingness takes its place. The thought comes rumbling through: "Was this your idea, or mine?" An answer reverberates: "Who wants to know?" Silent laughter shimmers through the space.

A change occurs in the quality of communication. It is no longer an exchange of thought, but a kind of self-communication, all occurring internally within the being. Along with this comes the hilarious shock of recognition: love is self-love, because there is no other. The ultimate ego-game.

They remain passive. There is nothing that needs doing here. They allow everything to go by without resistance. As their collective consciousness settles into this space they become aware of being the entire content of the universe. In the beginning of this state they can see themselves as the Primordial Being, twisting and turning in the early shock stages of beingness.

Around them now there is nothing whatever to feel or to sense. They cannot at this moment see any action within the universe.

They seem to be automatically forming a matrix of complex spatial connection, created from simple repetitive design. Each star of the now visible universe forms one cell of this cosmic body. They have become a mandala. As they look inside, they are able to see great swirling masses of stars and galaxies.

There is a quality of endless waiting. The initial discomfort which began during the mixing and swirling stage has given way to a sensation of euphoric well-being. The swirling has stopped for a moment, and a state of complete stillness descends upon them. Everything is poised, as if on the brink of a Great Event. The universe seems to be holding its breath.

They observe the formation of a point of light in the distance. They watch as it enters into the crystalline web between the stars, disappearing into the fabric of the universe. They watch several more of these as they, too, form and vanish into the matrix of space.

Eventually they separate into two entities once again in order to begin the space-game. They select identities and move apart with the simultaneous command to withdraw.

They become aware once again of themselves as human beings. Slowly they separate from the co-motion of the Cosmic Couple. Their bodies remain very still. They assume their bodies slowly so that they are not damaged by re-entry. They allow their bodies to remain motionless for a while longer until the assimilation of consciousness is complete. Then they slowly disengage. They have been reborn into the world.

OBJECTIVE SEX WORKSHOP — STUDENT REPORTS

Student Experiences

First Couple:

"The main thing we felt was an expansion of space and a peaceful stillness. We heard other sounds besides our heartbeats and nervous systems, but we didn't know what they were.

One sound in particular was a booming reverberation off in the distance and then it would get closer and recede again.

We also felt a swirling sensation when we did the Humming Mantra. When we returned to BodySpace we felt quite different than we had before starting.

We were able to get into MetaSpace easily, but at first got all kinds of body sensations such as itching, being generally uncomfortable and wanting to move around to adjust for muscle tension.

At first there was a certain amount of noise

from other participants in the workshop, which kept throwing us off until about halfway through. Then we didn't hear any outside noises at all.

We got a lot of phenomena such as peculiar sounds, lights flashing at intervals, and the sensation of our bodies twisting sideways and bending into unusual shapes even though we weren't moving.

Then we got an awareness of a source of white light coming from above and slightly to the side. It got brighter, then dimmer, but it stayed visible all the time. We felt a slight fear that we might become lost in the light, but nothing like that happened.

The next memory was of a decision "We'll need some sort of body here in this space." Then we dropped into BodySpace and it was the end of the exercise. Some sort of internal clock must have been operating that made us aware that the exercise was over.

We weren't asleep at the end, but there was one period neither of us can remember clearly. We got the feeling at some points that there wasn't anything we could do anyway, so we just let ourselves be nothing in particular."

Second Couple:

"Almost immediately upon entering MetaSpace we started to take on different bodies, some of which were animal forms. Each one lasted only for a moment. As soon as the sensations of being that type of body hit us we felt pulled back to our human forms.

Then we got a lot of mental chatter and visual phenomena such as lights and ripples of lightning.

Then we saw a kind of sunset scene. There was a source of light hidden behind a mound or sand-dune. Then the dune started rolling toward us and we got out of there.

The next memory is of moving straight up toward a latticework of white lines on a black background. We were rushing towards it and then slowed down just before we reached it. The latticework lines faded and we found ourselves in a blackout period.

We do not feel that we fell asleep, but whatever happened to us after that blackout is outside our present ability to recall. At some point after this incident we got into body awareness and returned to BodySpace.''

Third Couple:

''Nothing out of the ordinary happened, although body sensations were heightened. There was a great deal of energy flow in the form of pressure and some burning sensations upward along the spine, some pressure at the forehead as if the sinus cavities were about to explode.

We were pretty much nonreactive to body sensations being familiar with them from previous meditation, but we did feel a wee bit of concern over the numbness in the upper backs and throats.

We automatically held our breath and stopped the Humming Mantra for a while to channel energy upward. It was nice to experience this but no different from our ordinary meditation.

We were able to maintain our position for the full exercise period without getting too tired. Pretty much a nonthinking state although we were fully aware of what was happening around us including some far away sounds of thunder.''

Fourth Couple:

''Body sensations of pressure and heat. Mental chatter increased at first, but in time the sensations and chatter dropped off by themselves.

A timeless and nonremembering state ensued until very shortly before the end of the exercise. At this point we saw a brilliant light, and assumed that it was a warning to go back to BodySpace, that we weren't ready for this. So we used the re-entry meditation and came back into our bodies. Maybe next time.''

Fifth Couple:

''Some fragmented mind trips and energy flowed up. Mostly we were a nothingness lapsing in and out of being something or other.

We weren't making any attempts to do anything or to remain attentive to anything in particular.

There was a period of super tiredness, disinterest and slight depression at the end when we realized that we would have to go back into our bodies again, but we came back anyway.''

Sixth Couple:

"We went completely numb and broke through into a space in which we seemed to be pushing energy around. We heard something like laughter or talking in a high-pitched voice or voices, but we couldn't see where it was coming from.

The breathing became shallow and we finally hit a space where we weren't breathing at all. We were there for what seemed like a long time. The shock of release from that space sent us spinning into another space in which we got a lot of visual phenomena.

We felt as if we were turning over and over while the body arched and the backs of our heads touched our spines at the base. It felt as if we were being molded into this shape by something else.

It felt as if we were falling endlessly through space and we both got a little frightened. We held on, though. We had thoughts about missing the morning class if we got lost.

At some point we did a swan dive accompanied by some kind of an internal shriek which was emitted from the throat area, but there was no sound. We melted into a wall and then it got dark. Near the end of this experience an arm seemed to pull us forcibly into BodySpace.

Our thought was: "Now it's time to get out of this space. Someone else wants to use it." The arm disappeared at that time so we shook ourselves loose from that space and sat up. The coach asked us what we were doing, coming out of it so fast. So we allowed ourselves to drop back into position and come back more gently.

Everything felt very humorous and we laughed when normal perception and sensation returned."

Seventh Couple:

"Flying sensations at first. Got into a space in which everything was airless. We didn't like it. It felt very stuffy and dangerous.

It got very cold on our backs. We felt out of balance and wanted to adjust position, but didn't break it.

Mental programs kept interfering. Suddenly got a tremendous burst of energy through the chest and back, finally let go and just floated around.

We moved into a few new spaces and found some barriers which we will try to overcome next exercise session. Very confident that we can break through with practice. The whole thing is getting much easier. Sensations are not bothering us as much as they did at first."

Eighth Couple:

"Magnificent sense of isolation, great comfort. Slow breathing and pulse rate felt very good. We went up and down the sensory scale, occasionally being jarred into new and different spaces. Far off we heard a woman's voice calling to us and thought it might be the coach.

Forms began to appear in which we seemed to be in a court of a king. We heard a voice giving a running commentary which reminded us that there are five courts of five kings. Instantly transported to something called the "new court". In comparing notes, we found that we each heard the same things.

Then a rapid swirl through stars and galaxies toward some distant goal. Blacked out before this goal was reached and remember nothing more until returning to BodySpace.''

Ninth Couple:

"We were very busy with considerations about being here, memories, chatter, money problems.

The atmosphere got warm and we began to spiral downward. Then we fell into BodySpace and realized the whole reality we thought we had been into was not the everyday reality.''

Tenth Couple:

"A lot of body sensations at first, then visual phenomena and sounds. Got impatient and discouraged, but right after that we broke through.

A white light came from nowhere and hovered above us for a while. Then it faded out. We felt quite fearful of our inability to find our way back again if we got lost, but this feeling went away after a while.

The space we got into looked a little weird at first, but then we got very relaxed. Felt very calm and peaceful. Looked like Middle Earth.

At the end there was some kind of cave with a book of records beside the entrance. Cats were walking around on hind legs. Then a sound came from far away and we realized that it was time to end the session.''

Eleventh Couple:

"Began with the idea of looking at resistances in our relationship and finding out what they were all about.

But suddenly we broke through into MetaSpace and began spinning. Then the spinning stopped. We went out cold and don't remember a thing until we came back into BodySpace. Had a feeling of heightened sensitivity to each other and still have it an hour later."

Twelfth couple:

"All body tension at first. Restlessness from lying down too much today. Visualized ourselves as a jellyfish.

Then suddenly we were exploded into a space in which we were a galaxy of shooting stars. We forgot all about body and went with it.

At one point we thought we were sitting at a table eating some barbecued ribs, but then realized that it couldn't possibly be happening, and just as suddenly, it wasn't.

We found ourselves floating in some kind of sticky pudding. Moving was impossible and it was all around us, boxing us in.

The sound of our hearts beating became so loud we couldn't concentrate on anything else.

We got a sense of disorientation, and then relaxed. Just as we relaxed, a giant wave hit us and left us gasping for breath.

A blue mist began to permeate the space, and we

saw someone coming toward us. Just before he got to where we were there was a rumbling sound and a thrust of energy poured through us. Then wham! Back to BodySpace.''

Thirteenth Couple:

"This time we were not going to pamper ourselves. Upon breaking through BodySpace we felt a strong sense of permanence which gave us a good feeling of confidence.

We felt very much our own selves and acknowledged that we were going to go all the way with this. We knew that if we wanted to, we could simulate our own experience.

We began to experience an opening and closing like that of a clam. Then it felt as if we were a beautiful flower opening and closing its petals. There seemed to be no exit from this space. "We're stuck," we thought. We silently asked for the Guide's help in getting us back to our bodies.

We thought we were back and that the workshop was over. We packed our things and went home. Then we found ourselves back in MetaSpace again. This happened several times.

We became rather paranoid. Fear of not getting back to BodySpace, not knowing which reality was the real one, fear of acknowledging the fear programs.

In a moment of extreme doubt we jetted out of that space into a new space in which we saw a pair of eyes. Every now and again there would materialize wonderful ballets of blue and green electricity. At points we became quite frustrated because the Guides were not appearing. Then we got pushed into a small space in which we could see a blazing triangle of light. We felt as if we were floating on the surface of the ocean, gently being pushed this way and that by the waves.

It got dark and there were occasional flashes of light. Then finally we saw the Guides and they moved toward us. They led us out of the dark space into another space in which everything glittered and light ran up and down the sides.

We heard a heavy rumbling sound coming from above, and rays of light began to blast through us and we started to float upward as though supported by bubbles below.

Dark clouds formed above us, changing their shapes rather quickly from one to another. They began dancing and after a bit of spinning and falling during which we turned head over heels things quieted down.

After a while we began to hear voices, first one, then many. We saw a few faces talking very loudly in a rasping way. When we saw them we laughed and said, ''Okay, you can be our Guides.''

The high babble of voices and energy became distracting and we started to get involved with the trips and began to hold conversations with the voices. The babbling voices became a turbulent layer above us that we could hear clearly and could be aware of, but which had nothing to do with us. We could be free of it if we wanted to.

We saw an ancient corroded face before us which drew us out to the stars.

With a lurching sensation we found ourselves in a

black space in which we got very beautiful sensations of complete freedom. It was all right to be there without worrying about the passage of time and with just a very remote idea of ourselves existing as forms.

There was a feeling of being with friends and although we could see no one, we could feel the closeness of others, whoever and whatever they were.

It seemed strange to break this timeless condition and come back to this cramped and painful space and be inside a body again. We did not want to come back, but something got us to. We would like to find out what keeps dragging us back in to BodySpace. Did we actually come back to BodySpace or will we suddenly find ourselves back in MetaSpace again?

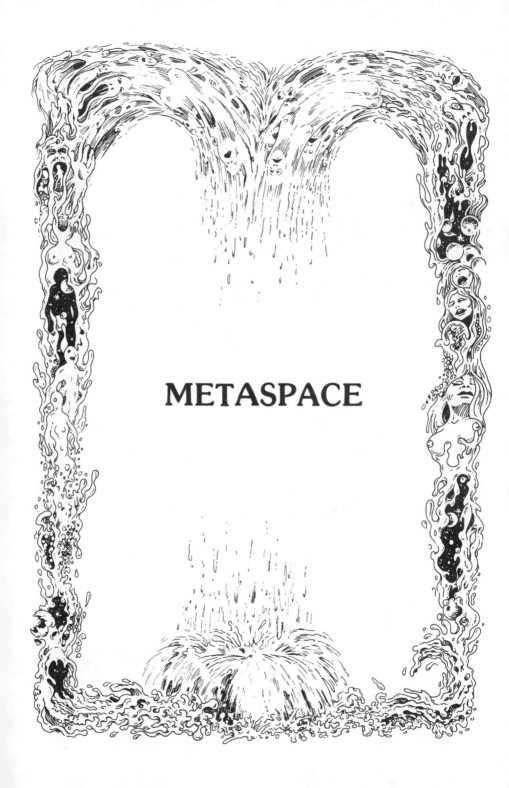

METASPACE

Metaspace

MetaSpace, the Center of the Void, is the most important "space change" occurring in Objective Sex.

It is the result of going beyond BodySpace. Recognition of MetaSpace is important, because by knowing that one is in MetaSpace one will know that BodySpace has been transcended.

One must be able to recognize MetaSpace. MetaSpace is perceived by its phenomena.

The Key to recognizing the phenomena of MetaSpace is that if it is happening to you, it is simultaneously happening to your partner. In other words, if a change occurs in your perception, you can be certain that your partner is seeing it the same way, because you are both sharing the same space.

At first one may only have momentary experiences of MetaSpace, but these will eventually stabilize and with practice one will attain the ability to increase the length of time spent together in MetaSpace.

Phenomena of MetaSpace:

1. Everything gets brighter, as if lighted from within.
2. Vision becomes sharper, but objects appear fuzzy and far away.
3. Colors and sound are more intense. Everything seems to be an extension of yourself.
4. The walls are alive. All objects seem to have being of their own.
5. Everything seems delicate and exquisite; poised with expectation. The atmosphere is sweet and fragrant.
6. There is a feeling of euphoria. One wonders if one still has a body.
7. There is a feeling of friendliness about everything.
8. There is an urge to chuckle at how the universe is constructed and the part you play within it.
9. There is a feeling that you know something Great, but Inexpressible.
10. There is a great release of heat and sometimes laughter, as soon as one accepts being in this space.
11. Infinity ends abruptly about ten feet away.

THEORY OF
OBJECTIVE SEX

Theory of Objective Sex

In order to understand what happens during Objective Sex it is necessary to understand the relationship between ordinary consciousness, or the *Psyche*, and the Superconsciousness — which is the awakened un-conscious — called *Essence*.

It is Essence which represents the Deep Self, not the Psyche. We will begin by defining these words to see how the definition may help one to clarify and understand them.

The Essence, or Deep Self, is composed of 18 Primordial Habits. These automatic programs do not depend upon any external influences for their existence. These habits are the only part of consciousness and identity which survive death. The Essence is also called the *Body of Habits*.

Under optimum conditions the habits contained in Essence should automatically create the impulses to live a conscious life, to take only the Higher Rebirths, and to awaken in each life.

In most individuals the habits composing the Essence have accumulated at random, thus creating impulses to take rebirth in lower forms, collect possessions, aggressively extend power, and live in fear and ignorance. What has happened to make this come about?

Habits accumulate naturally from one's experience in time and space. Ordinarily time/space experiences should have no effect on the Body of Habits, but in order to attain this immunity one must have crystallized the Seventh Higher Being Body. If this has not occurred, the habits contained in the Essence can be accidentally replaced by habits accumulated from time/space experiences. These time/space habits tend to be survival and pleasure oriented.

Survival doesn't care how you survive. It has integrity only in the matter of survival. It provides no opportunity for the evolution of the Essence, because it has no use for conscience and compassion.

One can call this collection of unconsciously accumulated habits Essence, Karma, DNA, the Soul, or the Transit Guide. Through the action of this Body of Habits one is helplessly compelled to dramatize the same things, to form the same personality, and to relate to the same types of individuals again and again. One is doomed to endless and eternal repetition until these Basic Habits are replaced by Conscious Habits. This cannot happen accidentally or through outside influences. This endless repetition of life is called the Wheel of Karma or Recurrence.

How does this affect one's life? During periods of stress, the Essence becomes the controlling mechanism, because no other entity can be present at that time.

In ordinary calm periods, one is controlled by — and identifies oneself as — the psyche. The psyche is also composed of habits, but they do not survive during stress. They are the Minor Habits, created and programmed by social and cultural conditioning. Here one finds the habits of eating, sleeping, breathing, thinking, moving, gender and social roles, memory and body perceptions, and language — among others. The psyche is the mind, plus the body, plus the nervous system, not including the muscle system. The muscle system is the physical manifestation of the Essence.

During stress, the psyche is forced to close down. At this time the muscle system rules the organism, acting as a very simple survival mechanism.

In ordinary life the psyche dominates the Essence, because life seems very complex, and the Essence is too simple to handle it. There is a moment during which the Essence gives control of the organism over to the psyche. This is called the *Great Self-Betrayal*.

When a period of stress occurs, the psyche closes down. Stress produces large amounts of electricity through the nervous system. The psyche is not built to handle large voltages. It isolates itself until the emergency is over.

Essence handles emergency conditions because it is able to function under the high voltage generated by the body during stress states. It is programmed to survive by copying earlier actions that worked to help it survive. The action may be wildly inappropriate now, or even harmful, but it will stupidly repeat some past action that worked before, *just because it worked before.*

If one observes oneself while under severe stress one can see why this subject should be of concern to anyone wishing to experience Objective Sex.

Under ordinary conditions of life, the actions, attitudes and experience of the Essence will be anything *but* conscious. And yet Essence is the identity with which one will experience sex, because *sex induces a high-stress state.*

When one becomes aware of the existence of deep programming — contained in the Body of Habits — one usually wishes to immediately replace them with "good" habits. But without knowing what to change one may make it even worse than before.

One may then decide to eliminate all habits. But one cannot eliminate habits. Habits *are* the Essence — the Deep Self. One cannot remove the self from the self.

It is valuable to alter the Essence along conscious lines, but this can only be accomplished through reaching and altering the deep levels of programming in the muscles and moving-instinctive center.

Most people fear their Essences. They spend their lives in futile searches to avoid stress, thus enhancing the psyche and keeping it in control. But perhaps this is better than running amok. Various forms of self-calming are used in modern cultures to prevent the accidental breakdown of cultural programming.

Of course this completely prevents the development of the Essence, because if it is not exposed, it is not open to learning or to reprogramming. Certain kinds of stress are good for replacement of habits while others are not. For example, the stress induced by drugs is a method of replacing habits, but substitution occurs on a random basis and generally reinforces the original conditioning. Thus one may do terrible harm to the Essence. If the Essence is at all disposed to Work on itself and toward its development, it is best not to tamper with it until one knows how to repair the machine.

Essence is hidden beneath the veneer of the psyche because it would be hard for most people to function simply. It would be embarrassing to be temporarily unable to read, write or talk. Essence may have shut down at a very early age, leaving one barely able to do more than open the mouth and suck milk from a nipple.

Many yogis and fakirs who suddenly destroy their psyches manifest this condition.

It is possible to *pre-train the Essence* to be able to function without the direction of the psyche. It is this *pre-breakdown training* which comprises the method called the *Sly Path*. Instead of becoming a helpless baby, one is then able to *do*.

Through the intentional use of *stress factors* the Essence can be exposed on a more or less permanent basis. This special type of stress is caused by intentional struggle with the self and with one's nature. It is a battle between higher and lower centers, each of which have different goals.

Many people think that Buddha sat under the Bodhi tree to relax, or that meditation is a refuge from stress. This is opposite from the truth. The technique of meditation — or 'sitting quietly' — is to create a struggle with the desire for external and internal stimulation.

Only by continuous struggle is it possible to open the Essence and make the delicate changes necessary for conscious life. If the Essence remains buried beneath the obscuring force of the psyche, no real change in the Being is possible. The mind may change, the personality may change, basic behavior patterns may change, but there is no lasting change. Everything will be the same as before.

Even if one is willing to create stress for oneself, it usually takes a negative form. Instead of using correct stress factors, one may prefer more pleasurable stress factors. Thus one may use subjective art, expressive dance or music, and calming meditations as 'stress factors'.

Development along mental and physical lines may seem like a good idea while in life, because one wishes to be successful and comfortable. For most people this kind of success is sufficient, and they don't mind the endless cycle of repetition, because they don't remember it.

When one has learned through The Method — using intentional stress factors, one of which is Objective Sex — to replace the automatic habits of Essence with conscious habits, one will have brought the body, mind and emotions into a usable form. Then one is ready to begin Real Work — the Crystallization of Higher Bodies.

BEGINNING
EXERCISES

Beginning Exercises

EXERCISE ONE: SERENITY

During the course of your ordinary sex, have a conversation as if you were doing something completely different.

Use a calm flat voice, with no inflections, grunts, groans or oohs and aahs.

Do not attempt to bypass the orgasm, but when orgasm occurs, be calm, serene and relaxed. If you can't manage that yet, try being bored with the orgasm. Relax the stomach and abdominal muscles before and during orgasm. This is very important.

EXERCISE TWO: WHITE RABBIT

Sit upright, the male with legs crossed or in lotus

position, female seated over, legs wrapped around his hips or waist. Maintain this contact while you have a conversation about something imaginary.

Example:

> "Say, did you just see a white rabbit?"
> "You mean the one with a gold pocket watch?"
> "Yes."
> "Was he wearing checkered trousers and a waistcoat?"
> "Yes, yes, that's it exactly!"
> "This rabbit — was he muttering something about being late for an important date?"
> "Yes, that's him!"
> "Sorry, never saw him!"

EXERCISE THREE: FRIARS' CLUB

Sitting upright as in Exercise Two, look into each other's eyes, relax the face mask, relax the abdominal muscles.

Now tell each other jokes. Try not to laugh and deliver the punchlines in as flat a tone as possible.

Instead of laughing, just say that it was funny or not funny. Alternate the joke telling if you wish, first one partner, then the other. This is very good for getting off most of the social conditioning about sex.

Example:

> "Did you ever hear the one about the traveling salesman?"

"Yes."
"Well, I'm going to tell it anyway."
"All right, go ahead."
"There was this traveling salesman who lived on an island...." [etc.]
"That was extremely funny. Now I'll tell you one."

EXERCISE FOUR: PICKUP

During the course of your ordinary sex create a conversation as if you had just met and were standing on a streetcorner or in a room crowded with people — say, at a party.

Example:

"Hi, what's yer sign?"
"Keep Off."
"Hold on, I wasn't trying to pick you up. I thought you looked familiar."
"Uh huh....Sure, sailor."

EXERCISE FIVE: TOM JONES

Go to a restaurant or some other public place and *quietly* create a conversation as if you were engaged in wild lovemaking, but just sit quietly and eat your food as you carry on this conversation.

Be quiet enough about this that your neighbors at the next table don't get upset. It isn't okay to involve unwilling participants in your trip.

Example:

"Ooooh, that's good. Oh, do it again."
"Yeah, baby, wow."
"Grunt, groan, uhhh."
[for examples you might read Zap Comics.]

Of course during this verbal dramatization you are seated quietly, reading the menu, eating, ordering food, and so forth, acting as casual as possible. Look bored, almost totally disinterested in what you are saying, but make it sound real, using an underbreath tone to carry the sensuous emotional impact.

EXERCISE SIX: SHARING SPACE

Sitting opposite each other, cross-legged on a bed or on the floor, no physical contact.

Do not try to do anything or be anyone with each other. Just think of yourselves as two Beings who have been with each other for so many billennia that there's nothing left to say or do, because it has all been said and done before.

Don't fall asleep or get into daydreaming. Stay strictly away from head trips.

Above all, don't give in to the urge to smile, amuse yourselves or each other, apologize for being there by being funny or cute, or be interesting. When you sit together in this exercise, think of it as a double asana in which you do not move until the exercise is completed.

If you laugh or break up, start over. This asana should be done for at least fifteen minutes without breaking. (laughing, moving or falling into daydream or headspace is considered a break.)

Your eyes are open and focused on your partner's eyes throughout this exercise. If possible, focus beyond your partner's eyes into the space of the Being behind the eyes.

EXERCISE SEVEN: EGO TRIP

Sitting opposite each other, deliberately hold a continuous smile. As you smile, and with plenty of drama, tell and show your partner how wonderful you are, and why you are wonderful.

Take turns at this, five minutes each, with a five minute break for relaxation of the facial mask. Only the partner doing the talking should be holding the smile. The other partner just listens and silently acknowledges everything that is said.

Make up things about yourselves if necessary. In fact, it is even more fun if you do make it up, as if you never really existed.

EXERCISE EIGHT: RIDICULE

Still holding that smile and sitting opposite each other, tell each other what rotten finks you are. Taking turns, each partner says why they are not wonderful. This should be self-invalidation, not invalidation of your partner.

Don't hold back just because it isn't true, and you really are wonderful. Again, making these things up will be much more fun than using real things. You can use a certain amount of coaching. Here is an example of how one partner can coach the other:

Example:

> "Tell me a lie about yourself."
> "I threw a manhole cover on a watchdog yesterday."
> "Okay. Tell me a lie about yourself."
> "I flew over the roof of the building across the street and just as I was floating down I passed a rooster on his way up."
> "Okay, tell me another lie about yourself"...and so on.

The funnier you make it, the easier it will be. You should continue this exercise until it is easy for you to make up things about yourself, and especially until you can make up "bad" things about yourself.

This is a good exercise for strengthening the ability to stand apart from one's trips, attitudes and the need for self-validation. A great spine-relaxer.

EXERCISE NINE: MONOTONY

Whenever you are together, after work or whatever you do apart from each other, just be there without having to amuse each other or yourselves.

Don't talk, don't watch TV — just be together. Do this for a full week during the times when both of you are at home.

Do not use magazines, newspapers, radio, TV, books or other people to provide amusement or to relieve boredom.

You should be able to be with each other for a week without having to amuse or be amused.

Don't get into story telling, charades or grinning just to break it for a moment.

If this drives you up the wall, you might re-evaluate your relationship.

Do not get grim or turned-off. It is important to enjoy just being together, to remain alive and interested, even when nothing is happening.

You might even grow to like it, and want to do this for one day each week. Fasting from words is just like fasting from food. Once in a while it is a good thing, to revitalize and re-energize the inner life.

You might even wonder how you allowed all these distractions to come between you in the first place. This exercise can be extremely habit-forming. You might even end up selling your TV.

LOOKING AT YOUR RELATIONSHIP

It is important to fully understand the scope and the limits of relationship in order to develop the free exchange of self and identity between you and a partner in states beyond BodySpace. Here is a method of looking at the dynamics of your relationship.

1.   What is important about this relationship? (Make a list).
2.   How are you helping this relationship to work?
3.   How are you opposing this relationship?
4.   How much effort does this relationship require now?

5. How much effort are you willing to give this relationship in the future?
6. On a scale of one to ten, with one at the top, what priority do you place on each of the following?

    1. Yourself
    2. Your lover
    3. Other people
    4. Your home
    5. Sex
    6. Love
    7. Your family
    8. Your work
    9. Your play
    10. Your spiritual development
    11. Pleasure
    12. Your desires
    13. Objects
    14. Wealth or social standing.

INTERMEDIATE
EXERCISES

Intermediate Exercises

EXERCISE ONE: WHERE IS IT COMING FROM?

Sitting opposite each other, looking directly into each other's eyes, slowly repeat together:

"I....I....I...."
"You....You....You...."
"God....God....God...."

Notice that each sounding of these words seems to come from a different place in or around your body. Decide as you vocalize each word just exactly where that sound reverberates or at which point it is centering.

Example:

"I...." (in the center of the head)
"I...." (in the head again)
"I...." (now it's in the throat)
"You...." (behind the eyes)
"You...." (behind your eyes)
"You...." (just for a moment it was in my heart)
"God...." (that's reverberating just above my head)
"God...." (behind me)
"God...." (all around us)

Next, decide where you want to make the sound of the word reverberate, and have it center there. On the third pass through this exercise, sound each word silently and notice where it reverberates. This third part may take some practice before you get it to work.

EXERCISE TWO: FLOWING IN A SINGLE FORM

Interlock your bodies and lie back forming a single body with a head on each end.

During this exercise it is important not to move, once in position.

At first simply extend your attention over your own body, running your awareness up and down, separating the sensations of your body from your partner's body. Feel and sense your own body.

Now begin to allow your body sensing to flow into your partner's body, sensing that body as if it were part of your own. Accept the feelings and sensations of your partner's body, no matter what it feels like to you. Most important, accept that it is possible to do this.

Connect the sense of being in both bodies at once, and flow your awareness through both bodies as if they were a single form. See yourself as having one large body with four arms, and a head at each end.

EXERCISE THREE: FLOWING VARIATION, UPRIGHT

Do the same exercise as in Exercise Two, but sit upright instead of lying down.

Hold the wrists in locked position, relax the back and neck muscles, and drop the facial mask.

It helps to close the eyes or to press the foreheads together. When the foreheads are pressed together you will see the "One Eye Love".

EXERCISE FOUR: STILLNESS AND CONTROL

Part One:

Allow only one inch of penetration. Hold this steady.

Remain absolutely still, as if in an asana, breathe normally. Relax any tension as it builds up. The face mask and neck muscles are the most likely to tense.

Remain in this position for five minutes and then break without any further sexual action or stimulation. Don't apologize for not completing intercourse. It is complete.

Part Two:

Several days after this, having had no sexual contact between-times, do it again, this time remaining in the motionless state for ten minutes and then breaking without further contact. The male partner should not be concerned with maintaining an erection or penetration at this stage.

Part Three:

Several days afterward, again do this exercise, this time holding the steady state described in part one for one half hour to a full hour, depending on your physical and emotional endurance.

Only those sexual contacts as outlined above should occur during this exercise, which is spread over a period of nine or ten days.

EXERCISE FIVE: BREAK CONTACT CONTROL

During the course of your ordinary sex, break contact before either of you is able to have an orgasm.

Immediately withdraw physical contact, quietly get dressed, and do something else together. Anything but sex.

Do not return to sexual contact for at least twenty-four hours. If you become upset, frustrated or disappointed, find out where those attitudes and beliefs come from.

Notice that as a Being you consider sex to be complete whether or not an orgasm occurs.

Your animal soul is the part of you that does not consider sex complete without an orgasm, and your body's survival urges are the basic drive for orgasm below that level of programming.

This exercise helps to develop will power in bypassing the orgasm, an important ability in Objective Sex.

EXERCISE SIX: ALMOST

Go through all the motions and preparation for sex, including extensive foreplay and stroking.

Just before contact, stop and back off for one full hour.

Time this by watching a clock or the second hand on a watch. Time it to the exact minute.

After one hour, proceed as if nothing had occurred in the interim. Note any changes in attitude as a result of this exercise, and discuss these with your partner.

It is vital that the genitals do not touch, even for a single moment, in the first part of this exercise.

You might count off the seconds when the last minute ticks off on the clock.

EXERCISE SEVEN: CONTROLLED BREATHING

Seated opposite each other, breathe slowly in and out in the normal manner, but adjust slightly so that when you breathe in, your partner is breathing out.

You should be seated no more than two feet away from each other, and looking directly into each other's eyes.

Do this for fifteen minutes and then take a break. Make sure your breathing remains smooth and gentle, not ragged or forced.

Never radically alter your breathing unless working with a fully trained breath coach.

EXERCISE EIGHT: COSMIC COUPLE

Seated opposite your partner, imagine each other to be the other half of the Cosmic Couple.

Describe aloud your partner's cosmic qualities. Use a lot of form and color in your description. It doesn't have to be the same description twice.

Example:

"You have a blue body. Your eyes are very large. You have four heads and eight arms. I can see ripples of lightning over your eyebrows."

It is best to turn out the lights and do this exercise in the dark. Keep your eyes open.

EXERCISE NINE: CONCENTRATION

Each of you sits in front of a candle.

Place your visual attention just above the tip of the flame. Look for an etheric flame just above the physical flame. When you can see it, pull it down over the physical flame until they both disappear for a moment, cancelling each other out.

Bring the etheric flame back up and slowly

withdraw your attention from the candle. Close your eyes and take a "cleansing breath", slowly exhaling. Relax for a few minutes before attempting it again. Do this several times, until you can easily cancel the physical flame with the etheric flame.

EXERCISE TEN: CATEGORIES

Sit opposite each other, about three feet apart. Place two objects of any kind between you.

One partner is the coach. The coach asks:"What is this?" The receiving partner must give an answer other than a human explanation for that object. Then the coach asks:"What is its use?" Again the receiving partner must answer other than in human explanations.

Then use the other object. Do this for ten full cycles, then switch roles.

It should take about two hours to fully explore non-human categories for two objects.

Example:

"What is this?" (Holding up a book)
"It's a Vortex Analyzer."
"What is its use?"
"It analyzes vortexes, of course."
"Oh, of course. (Picking up the other object) "And what is this?"
"That? That's a veeblefetzer"
"And what is its use?"
"It's used to fetz veebles...when you can catch them."

EXERCISE ELEVEN: SENSING EXERCISE

Seated quietly on the floor or on a cushion, note the shape of your body as if looking at a piece of sculpture. See the body only as a form in a particular posture or pose, not as a living organism.

This is a good exercise for combatting the desire to express negative emotions, and is done in the following way:

When in a negative state, never try to watch the mind or the emotions. They are too quick and one will be forever chasing them, like butterflies across a meadow.

The only way to turn negative states to positive material for self-knowledge is to use the moving center as a buffer. In this way the organism can be observed.

Simply observe the body as it dramatizes the state, watching it as one observes an actor upon the stage.

Do not try to stop it from manifesting. Just watch the physical actions. Pay no attention to the mental or emotional states which pass through the organism.

EXERCISE TWELVE: MELTING EXERCISE

Seated on the floor look just below the flame of the candle, at the blue part, or base of the flame.

As the wax melts, feel your body melting with it. After a while, when you feel that you want to stop the exercise, simply harden the body back to its original shape.

If necessary, use the sensing exercise to visualize the body's form in order to reconstruct it.

EXERCISE THIRTEEN: OPENING EXERCISE

Prepare for the exercise by lighting incense. Seated on the floor in a darkened room, imagine what it would be like for you if you had never existed. Now imagine what it would be like for those who relate to you as family, friends or lover.

Sit there until you can see yourself not existing, and then allow yourself to cease to exist for a moment or two, if you can.

Then allow yourself to exist once again, and end the exercise by rising and taking a cleansing breath.

THE ADVANTAGE OF SLOW BREATH

Rhythmic Slow Breathing is an essential element for Objective Sex. Used rhythmically, slow breathing brings the Solar Plexus to increased activity and makes possible the full tapping of Sex Energy from the Power Center. The radiation of this energy throughout the body breaks down the physical barrier to MetaSpace.

If the Humming Mantra is used in conjunction with the Slow Breath, the solar plexus is partially opened, thus developing it for later use in telepathic communication and Sharing, both necessary functions of perception for higher spaces where vocal communication and gesture communication are impossible.

MASTERING THE SLOW BREATH

*Keep the head up, abdomen pulled in and spine
straight while doing this exercise.*

1. Inhale through the nose, filling the lower part of
    the lungs, then the middle, then the upper.
    Make a special effort to fill the back part of the
    lungs as well as the customary front part.
2. As you breathe in, feel the finer life force
    contained in air being drawn in.
3. When the lungs have completely filled, begin to
    exhale, slowly contracting the chest, then
    emptying the back of the lungs, and then finally
    contracting the diaphragm in order to force out
    all the air possible. Bring all the muscles of the
    chest into this action, squeezing and contract-
    ing the chest as much as you can without
    discomfort.
4. During this exhalation process, feel the
    radiation of the finer spiritual body flowing
    outward through and beyond the physical body.
    Feel yourself as a transforming center of
    radiation for life force energy — as a source of
    higher vibration and transforming energy for all
    beings within the radius of your aura.
5. As the air is inhaled, pull the shoulders up
    slightly and lift the upper chest to assist the air
    intake, until it seems as if the air passage has
    filled completely. Very few individuals actually
    use the back part of the lungs, making true
    deep breathing impossible. One should make a
    good effort to use this back part of the lungs,
    even though it takes a little practice and
    attention.

6. When practicing breathing exercises, always remember to breathe rhythmically, and not to radically alter the breathing pattern. A good method of timing the rhythm of breathing is to practice at first during a walk. The walk will set the pace naturally, and one can achieve a good habitual pattern of rhythm in this way. Breathing rhythms are entirely individual, and thus no set rhythmic pattern or breath count per minute can be given for everyone. All breathing exercises should be adapted slowly and gradually — as well as carefully — to the individual's respiration rate, rather than by numbers of complete breaths per minute.

If this is done radically, incorrectly or if the breathing becomes ragged and off balance, other parts of the body can be affected. It is recommended that this exercise be done with a coach who has been thoroughly trained in teaching these types of exercises.

OPENING THE
SYMPATHETIC NERVOUS SYSTEM

Breathing is the Key to the Nervous System, and the Nervous System is in turn the Key to Higher Levels of Consciousness. Breath is the fire with which the Secret Mantras of the Inner Chambers are illuminated, and its mastery is called the Power of Meditation.

It is by the light of breath that one can see the Secret Mantras of the Great Mother, thus gaining access to higher and higher levels of consciousness.

In the body there are ten primary nerve channels of the *Sympathetic Nervous System*, which resonates with the other two main nervous systems, the *Central* and *Parasympathetic Nervous System*.

In the left side of the body, within the pleural membranes surrounding the lungs, is the Negative Section of the Sympathetic Nervous System. This left Section is called the "Holy Denying".

In the right side, surrounding the lungs, is the Positive Section of the Sympathetic Nervous System, called the "Holy Affirming".

Between them, where they interconnect like thin intertwined fingers is another section which operates in the same way as the locks in a canal. As the breath is inhaled, these channels open and close as energy is pulsed through them. This third section, which is the catalytic or neutralizing mechanism between the two main parts, is the *buffer* which makes possible the exchange of energy between the "Holy Denying" and the "Holy Affirming". This neutralizing section is called the "Holy Reconciling".

Ordinarily these channels are almost completely closed off and do not reverberate very much with the Central Nervous System. Most methods of breathing meditation and gymnastics are designed to open these up and enlarge them to the size necessary to pass sufficient energy to awaken the entire Nervous System.

Only by fully awakening and using the entire Nervous System is it possible to build a permanent bridge from BodySpace to MetaSpace.

Method:

1.   Body erect, spine straight, tip of tongue pressed

firmly against the roof of the mouth, begin the Humming Mantra with Slow Breathing, reverberating the Hum at the base of the palate and simultaneously in the abdominal region.

2. Push the reverberation of the Humming Mantra down through the air passages, from the mouth to the throat, to the solar plexus, to the abdomen, through the Holy Reconciling into the Holy Denying, going up the left side and passing once again through the Holy Reconciling into the Holy Affirming on the right side, down the right side to the base of the spine, back up through the center in the Holy Reconciling, all the way up to the base of the skull at the medulla oblongata, bouncing off the top of the head and ricocheting off the inside crown of the head through the pineal gland between the eyes at the root of the nose.

3. As it passes out of the body, pull the energy back down into the Power Center using the Mantra: "Ghaaaa!" Then begin again. Do this several times a day.

In the beginning, you will discover that your power of deep slow breathing is insufficient to accomplish the full circuit, but after a while you will be able to open the door to this Nervous System, and the channels will open and enlarge naturally, without effort.

In a few months you will be able to make the full circuit using the Humming Breath, thus reaching and opening the pineal gland, the so-called "Third Eye" of Essence Perception. At this time you should be able to see yourself from outside the body quite easily, and perceive externals without using the body's eyes.

Do this exercise gradually, allowing the breath to get stronger by itself. It is dangerous and unnecessary to force this exercise. After a while you will be able to get a breath one minute long.

It helps to trace the path of the energy and breath with the finger, as it moves through the Holy Denying, Holy Affirming, and Holy Reconciling parts of the Sympathetic Nervous System.

After a little practice, you will be able to naturally feel these currents moving through the system.

ENERGY FOR OBJECTIVE SEX

One ordinarily thinks of the tongue and mouth as instruments of speech and food intake. But there is another use for them which has the resulting effect of magnetizing the physical and etheric form, called "planetary" and "solar" bodies, respectively.

By pressing the tip of the tongue against the roof of the mouth the nerve energy from the solar plexus is released, shooting down along the nervous system.

This vibration reverberates in the muscles which begin sending out high voltages throughout the body. Thus the Power Center, which provides energy for Objective Sex, can be tapped. It cannot be opened or energy drawn from it in any ordinary way. No mental effort is sufficient to tap the force of the Power Center.

As a side effect of this action, one experiences an increase of resistance to external temperature changes, particularly to coldness. This effect on the body temperature control mechanism is called

"Dumo Heat".

Also, when the tip of the tongue is pressed firmly against the roof of the mouth, the passage from the sinus cavity to the lungs is enlarged, thus making it possible to fill the lungs more completely during slow breathing exercises.

HUMMING MANTRA

One can exercise the body muscles in gymnastics through physical effort, but one cannot exercise the brain in the same way.

Think of the brain as a musical instrument which you are about to tune through the use of sound. Also think of the brain as including the Central, Sympathetic and Parasympathetic Nervous Systems.

This is the first step toward really opening oneself up beyond BodySpace.

1. Hold the tongue firmly against the roof of the mouth.
2. Pull the abdomen inward and upward slightly without tensing.
3. Begin Humming, gently at first, then increasing in tempo and power.
4. Continue this exercise until you sense all parts of the body, including the cells, brain and nervous systems reverberating with the sound.
5. Then without vocalizing, make this same Humming Sound as if with the throat, until you can hear and feel the reverberation the same as when it was physically sounded.
It is useful to have a coach on this, to get the

precise pitch, tone and amount of nasal release. But any attempt is better than no attempt, and through practice one can usually realize the correct sound and create it.

"HUMN-YANGM-GHAAA"

One can practice this anytime during the day by making the sound while driving, walking or wherever one can do this without disturbing others. When this becomes impossible, use the silent mantra.

Anytime you feel a lack of energy or a decrease in power, practice this humming exercise. This will help you to remain in equilibrium and harmony.

If a mantra isn't reverberating, it isn't working.

"HUMN-HUMN-HUMN"

This mantra, done within the Humming Mantra, is used to build the Sex Energy to a peak. When one wishes to release the energy and return it to the Power Center, one simply exhales and sighs "Ghaaaaa!"

"HUNGA-LINGA"

This is a good Mantra for vibrating the Heart, but the exact pitch and tone are necessary. It is a rather high-pitched sound, and by experimenting, one can find the right pitch by sensing the body and noting when the solar plexus and heart reverberate with the sound.

It is also a good silent Mantra once the correct reverberating tone has been realized.

Technique For Getting Into Contact With Your Partner Using The Humming Mantra:

1. Sit erect opposite each other, holding eye contact.
2. Begin humming the mantra strongly, feeling its resulting reverberation in the body.
3. Begin to merge the two humming sounds until they resonate, then slowly decrease the level of sound, and finally only mentally hum the mantra.
4. Continue this exercise as long as the resonating effect lasts. Do this a few times each day, until it is possible to begin with the silent hum without the necessity for vocalizing.

This practice should be continued daily for a minimum of five minutes each cycle, four or five times daily for the first month, gradually increasing the number of cycles as you work toward MetaSpace.

MANTRA:

Every material object is a product of the combination of positive and negative impulses, combined with a catalyst — the third force — which keeps it in balance. This static form of combined forces is called "vibration". Vibration cannot occur without both positive and negative.

Through vibration the cosmic unformed substance can seem to have various forms, although in reality everything flows as one.

One seems to live within a dark chamber, inside the body, from which nothing flows and into which nothing flows. Because the body is a low vibration, it seems as if isolated — cut off — from the rest of the universal substance.

Consciously raising the vibration of the body and mind is the method of experiencing the flow of reality, thus bypassing the limits of consciousness imposed by the body.

One cannot raise the vibration of the body through the action of the mind. The low effect of passing thought through the body is to tense the muscles. The tension thus caused tends to age the cells. When one tries to relax outer layer muscles, although one has control over them through the mind, the effect is to increase the tension of the deeper layers, which are controlled by the involuntary nervous system.

These inner layers of muscle can be relaxed and their vibration increased to the level of the cosmic flow simply by using the appropriate body action.

It is possible to raise the level of vibration by combining the body action of Objective Sex with the method of attuning each center.

The goal of mantra is to vanish the body, by allowing its boundaries to dissipate into the universal substance, thus allowing one to flow into the cosmos without limitations or psyche obstructions. One becomes formless and ever-flowing, along with the universe as it is in reality. One expands directly into, and becomes a knowing part of, the single being which is both the life force behind the universe and the material world itself.

ASANA SCALE OF SENSATIONS

This scale is used for assuming a steady-state posture or position. The most important factor about asana is that one should find a posture that one can remain in for a long time without feeling compelled to adjust even the tiniest muscle for comfort or balance.

An asana does not necessarily have to be comfortable coming into it and going out of it, but one should be able to hold it indefinitely past the initial discomfort, and until the exercise is completed.

Every universe has its own shape. Different postures will suggest different universes. There are billions of possible spaces formed by asanas, because every alteration of muscle or body part, no matter how slight a change it is, creates a different space. Thus there are an almost infinite number of possible spaces one can enter through taking an asana up into its Prototype or Causal form.

Rather than give formal asana here, we suggest using your ordinary positions. This requires less adjustment to physical strain, leaving one free to notice the inner space changes and sensations while exploring higher spaces.

It is not necessary to use special positions for Objective Sex, although many people believe that this is so. Any position will work as long as it can be maintained without movement.

An asana is not attained until one is both still and completely relaxed. The scale of sensations will help you achieve this goal by taking you through all the intermediate stages one by one on a gradient level.

Why are formal asanas given? Formal asanas require that one assume an exact posture, even to the positions of fingers, toes and alignment of eyes, spine and head. They lead one into certain specific spaces in which knowledge is contained. This knowledge can only be transmitted to one while one is in those spaces. These asanas are only given by a teacher; they are never given publicly.

Therefore when one uses those already familiar positions, one is actually doing Karma Yoga, because one moves into those spaces which are available through habit.

The Key to asanas is to learn the Method for quieting the body. One never concerns oneself with the mind and emotions, for if the body is quieted, the mind and emotions automatically quiet themselves, too. This natural state will help one to direct one's attention on the attainment of MetaSpace.

The goal of asana is to park the body in a posture and have it remain still until one is finished exploring outside BodySpace. The asana is not achieved until this complete stillness has been attained.

One secret of achieving this stillness is to give up responsibility for moving the body. One can gradually give up responsibility for the body starting at the feet and working upward to the crown of the head.

As one moves into an asana, one moves through many levels of sensation before the actual attainment of the steady state. By following this Scale of

Sensations one can know from moment to moment how one is progressing toward attaining the completed form of the asana.

Scale of Sensations:

1. Put the body into posture and relax completely. Make certain no muscle tension is required to hold that position.
2. If necessary, now make any minor posture adjustments.
3. Once body adjustments have been made, no further movement should occur until the exercise is completed.
4. Major muscle layers are relaxed. First the outer, then the middle, then the inner layer. Use a Gray's anatomy or similar muscle chart to follow, or just do it by feel, sensing each muscle and allowing it to loosen. The body should not go out of balance during this procedure.
5. Close the mouth and breathe gently and slowly through the nose. If your breathing is ragged or sharp, take a Deep Cleansing Breath, and then begin again.
6. Drop the facial Mask. Check for tension in the corners of the mouth and the neck muscles.
7. Quiet the eye muscles. Check for tension at the temples, forehead and top of the jaws.
8. Relax the abdominal and stomach muscles. Once relaxed, these muscles should remain relaxed. Make certain they do not tense during the exercise.
9. Actively decide to refuse all impulses to adjust

your position, no matter what discomforts may arise. This affirmation will help you to remain in a good asana.

10. Close the eyes and unfocus the vision. (ordinarily the eyes focus even when the eyelids are closed.)
11. Surface muscles may begin to ripple slightly. Some myoneural discharge may occur.
12. A feeling of floating on clouds will occur. There may be a feeling of rotation or somersaulting.
13. The skin will begin to tingle. There may be some itchiness.
14. A sensation of floating in water. There will be a gentle pressure as if surrounded by water.
15. A feeling of motionlessness, as if in the ''eye'' of a hurricane. It may seem as if everything is whirling around one. This sensation, if also perceived, is called the ''Primum Mobile''.
16. One may wonder whether the body is still there.
17. A sensation of lightening, as the body of light separates into its etheric form.
18. Heaviness and a sensation of softening, like melting wax.
19. Tingling in the deeper levels, especially in the organs of the abdominal region.
20. A feeling of rising warmth, followed by clamminess in the limbs and lower back. Don't be concerned. Continue toward the asana — it has not yet been attained.
21. Breathing becomes very shallow, mouth becomes dry. Swallowing is almost unnecessary.

22. Heat begins to build in the upper crown of the head, and one feels as if one is above the body. This is where most people quit, but the asana has not yet been reached.
23. Another sensation of melting along with a sensation of slowly rocking back and forth, as if settling into mud.
24. A sensation of being absorbed into warm taffy or honey. This is the beginning of actually settling into the asana.
25. A sensation of fast vibration, sometimes preceded by a feeling of irritation or apprehension.
26. Be willing to remain in this space forever. Any desire for another space at this point will prevent the asana from occurring by making matching vibration inaccessible.
27. The stable vibration of the asana has been attained. One remains in this stable state until the exercise is completed. At this moment one is free to explore inner spaces.

SILENT REVERBERATION OF SYMPATHETIC NERVOUS SYSTEM

After one has practiced this for a while through the vocalization technique, it is possible to produce the same effect without manifesting the sound through the vocal chords.

At first it is helpful to close the eyes while reproducing the effect. Use sensing and feeling to help you re-produce this exercise. Soon just by vibrating the Sympathetic Nervous System you will be able to automatize this practice, making it a consciously created habit.

Your body will have attained an automatic method of maintaining harmony and will at the same time have achieved an automatic means of perfecting the higher bodies.

POWER MANTRA

In a way, powermantras are a throwback to the Early Days, when the energy from the Babylonian Light & Power Company wasn't sufficient to drive the Chakras by itself, and needed a little boost from innersound.

In fact, powermantras were discovered long before modern techniques of sound reproduction. The first mantras were nothing more than exponential concepts tuned to sound frequencies on the Causal Level, and intoned through the heart Chakra to boost the output.

As a result, some people scoffed at mantras, perhaps feeling that the science was regressing, when mantras were reintroduced by Paramahansa Yogananda in the fifties, and then by Maharishi, Nichiren Shoshu and Swami A.C. Bhaktivedanta in the early sixties.

Those early experimental Western mantras were pretty heavy, and after sounding them for a couple of hours your head felt as if it was going to sink down into your neck! But they did produce incredible effects, until the Babylonian Light & Power source was withdrawn, in 1972.

We had long been taught that to get good karma

from a mantra you had to increase the expansion factor of your limits by dropping old concepts and beliefs. But then along came Oscar Ichazo and his innovative nonconceptual resonance. The trick, of course, was that the diaphragm doesn't have to push around as much air as the back lungs. And if you get a good tight seal between the tongue and the palate, even the tiniest vibrations could produce a Transforming Effect.

Today there are about three hundred power-mantras, with *Sufi Sound & Remembering Exercises* the undisputed leader in the field. Sufi powermantras are custom-designed for the time, place and people, and are offered in just about every country in the world.

The first All-Centers Vivifying powermantras were really nothing more than miniature dynamic systems resonating in the solar plexus. But new methods of training and different non-physical approaches to sound reproduction have resulted in many advances. Some teachers have developed powermantras that can help you remain slightly away from your head (suspended by soft astral foam) and still get good sound reproduction without that closed-in feeling that shuts you off from the rest of the Real World.

Another new development comes from the pioneering Zen schools of Japan, which offer powermantras in two different categories. A signal applied to a thin, film-like membrane stretched between space and the Great Void, causing the inter-dimensional diaphragm to expand and contract simultaneously, pushing sound out into both the samsaric and nirvanic worlds at once.

One of the greatest advantages of powermantras is

that you need not be bothered by poor karma just because the body doesn't respond well to high-level sounds.

In that respect, powermantras are a little easier to select than ordinary verbal mantras, which often sound different at home than they did at the temple. But like ordinary mantras, powermantras must still be carefully auditioned by a coach, because each effect differs slightly according to one's pronunciation and emotional coloration.

Also, just like ordinary mantras, powermantras can be equipped with multiple driver energies, and some can be controlled to alter the balance between the light side and the dark side of The Force.

The increasing popularity of the powermantra has prompted one local teacher to introduce a combination system, in which a recording Witness is embedded in the nervous system. The idea is to permanently record space/time experience while in the body, using a self-contained simple-access akashic recording unit that can survive with the Body of Habits. When you play the recording back between lifetimes, you are treated to a high degree of spatial realism that has to be experienced to be believed.

A frequent complaint among students and seliks is that once they get into their astral bodies they're pretty much tied down to within a few million miles of the amplifying or transmitting body of light. But using powermantras, two schools have already developed astral bodies that don't require any cord at all. The astral self is sent out on the powermantra beam. Imagine being able to travel anywhere and still pick up signals and images from all the bodies you've ever run, even when you're in the still silence of the cosmic connection.

We've obviously come a long way since the writers of the Vedas were still trying to convince people to add just one more method to their transforming journeys.

Using Power Mantra

1.   Standing erect, heels together, hands dropped at the sides, lift the abdominal region up with some force, but short of discomfort.
2.   Inhale with a quick short breath, at the same time lifting the arms outstretched, forming the letter Y.
3.   Stand up on tiptoes, pulling the body up as far as possible.
4.   Now make a little extra effort to pull the body up even further.
5.   Press the second and third fingers of the hands against the thumbs, making the Sign of the Cat. Push the first and fourth fingers out straight.
6.   Chant the Humming Mantra, making the sound reverberate in the whole chest region, upper and lower.
7.   As you chant the Humming Mantra, slowly push the arms downward, but get the feeling that the body is rising upward through an opening in space.
8.   Continue this downward push and gradually

lower the arms down to the sides, pulling the abdominal area up and in.

9. Think of yourself as a Source of Life and Love Energy, standing in the Center of the Universe. Sing the Humming Mantra with the Power Tone. Decide to change the vibration rate of the body.
10. Become one with the Source of all Power.

TUNING IN TO THE SOUNDS OF METASPACE

1. Practice the Humming Mantra, resonating the sound in the nose, eyes, ears, roof of the mouth and throat — sinus cavities.
2. Listen with attention. As development of this listening ability increases, you will begin to hear sounds — These are the sounds of MetaSpace as heard from BodySpace.

Here are examples of some of the sounds you will begin to hear:
1. Swarm of Bees Buzzing.
2. A drumming sound, like hoofbeats.
3. Church bells.
4. Fire crackling.
5   Angelic choir.
6. Bagpipes.
7. Flute music.
8. Low muffled laughter.
9. Rolling thunder.
10. A volley of snaps and rolls.
11. A rushing wind.
12. Distant trumpeting.

13. High-pitched whine.
14. Watery sound.

PLANETARY VIBRATION

The vibration of the air and the subtle matter comprising the planetary sphere of earth varies considerably from hour to hour. The resulting body reverberation changes in accordance with planetary vibration, caused by relative position to the sun and other celestial bodies.

4 PM to Midnight — lowest
Midnight to 8 AM — highest

The best time for inner work, therefore, is the period between Midnight and 8 AM, utilizing the naturally higher vibration of the planet at that time.

JOURNEY THROUGH THE BODY UNIVERSE

As one performs this exercise, it is possible to supply life force, increased intelligence and love to each part of the body, directly into the cells, thus awakening the whole body to greater activity and power.

As one radiates love to each group of cells they will vibrate closer to perfect body health and harmony, just as plants do when love is radiated to them by a gardener.

Method:

Sitting erect in a chair, feet flat on the floor, with the fingers wrapped around the knees, think of the body as a great mansion in which are many special and separate rooms, each having a number. For the purpose of this exercise, divide the body into forty-nine rooms, seven associated with each of the chakras or body centers as listed below. To begin with, you may associate each room with a body part or organ, such as the arms, the throat, the stomach, the lungs, and so on. Later on, the rooms will take on their own character independent of their body association.

Keep in mind that visual and aural imagery is culturally relative, and specific images are given only as a guideline. By performing this exercise many times, you will develop the imagery of your own mansion experientially. For additional guidelines, you may consult the **American Book of the Dead** by E.J. Gold or an illuminated medieval Book of Hours.

Closing your eyes see yourself at the entrance to this great mansion, where your feet contact the floor or earth. See yourself about to enter room number one. You may associate this room with your feet, the next with ankles or calves, and so on moving upward through the body to the crown area.

Go into the first room for a few moments, sitting very quietly, listening and sensing the surroundings. Avoid making sudden movements or loud sounds in these rooms.

Feel the vibration of the room, at first slowly, then faster, then even more rapidly, as if hearing the gears shift in an automobile.

Then slowly get up and walk into the next room, room number two. With a feeling of projected love toward everything in the room, sit there quietly and become aware of its vibration, first slowly, then faster, then more rapidly.

In turn visit each room of the mansion and sense its unique vibration.

Now move through the opening at the top of the head, and see yourself outside the mansion. Always complete this sensing exercise by going to a point just above the head and remaining there for a few minutes, quietly observing the body below.

As you develop this exercise, begin to see yourself walking along the corridor from room to room, even forgetting the body name for each room, and just focusing on the number, vibration, colors and feeling of each room. After a while, you will begin to visualize personalities in each of these rooms. As they begin to appear, one should become familiar with them, conversing with them or simply sitting with them and enjoying their company. Also, every inhabitant of these inner rooms has something to teach, to impart. Thus knowledge can be attained by knowing these personalities dwelling in the forty-nine rooms of the mansion of Love.

Guidelines for Imagery of the Seven Chakras:

1. Your Foundation Center is the region below the genitals. Its symbol, the square, feels solid and permanent. Sense of smell increases in subtlety. Personalities you meet are friendly, familiar, like family. Color key is a yellow radiance or glow.
2. Your Abdominal Center is the region just above

the genitals. Its symbol, the crescent, expands in the center and tapers at the edges. Taste is stimulated. Personalities are friendly yet imposing, theatrical. Color key is the brilliant white of crystal chandeliers or stage lighting.

3. Your Navel Center is the diaphragm and solar plexus area. Its symbol, the triangle, expands from the center, diminishing in three directions. Sight is stimulated. Personalities are vivid and colorful. Color key is Red, a soft rosy glow.

4. Your Spinal Center is the heart and lungs area. Its symbol, the six-pointed hexagram, conveys unity and balance. Motion and touch are highlighted. Personalities flow and merge. Color key is smoky light, like candles or lamplight.

5. Your Upper Spinal Center is the neck and throat area. Its symbol, the circle, is expansive, deep, like vowel sound mantras. Awareness of space and its distortions is enhanced. Personalities are archetypes. Color key is the almost transparent yet vivid white of the void.

6. Your Forehead Center is the skull and third eye area. It has no symbol for its sense is perception itself. You see your own projections, perhaps with a sort of tunnel vision, gaining emotional insights. Personalities offer compelling messages. Color key is an absence of color.

7. Your Crown Center is at the top of the skull and beyond. Its symbol is the blossoming lotus or radiating sphere. When this center is open, the other chakras align and energy flows freely. Harmony, light and limitlessness are perceived. Large hosts of personalities radiate all colors. Color key is a radiating, shimmering blue white.

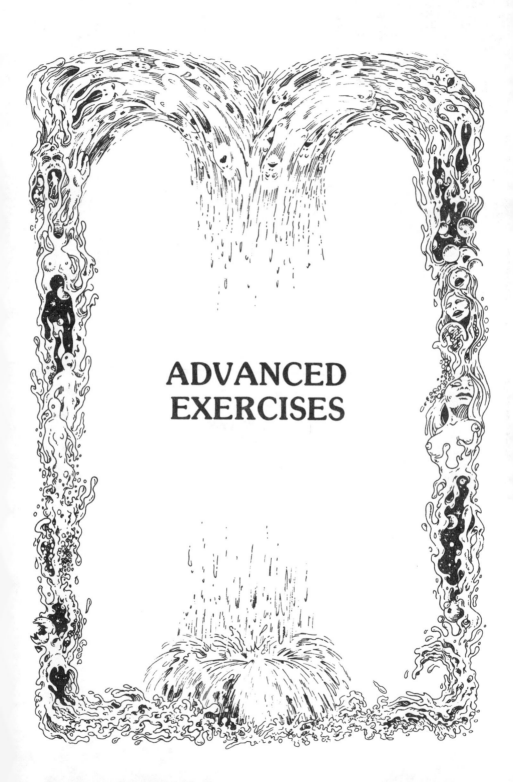

ADVANCED
EXERCISES

Advanced Exercises

OPENING THE SOLAR PLEXUS

By opening the solar plexus through the abdominal region one attains a tremendous increase in physical power and endurance. Then the Power Center can be opened. The other Centers will open by themselves through the continual use of the Power Center.*

The Solar Plexus is above the abdomen. This is the *Feeling Center*. Near the bottom of the spine is the *Power Center*, sometimes wrongly called the *Sex Center*. At the top of the spine is the *Thinking Center*. In addition to these three Centers there are three others which control *movement* and *speech*, *involuntary survival actions of the body*, and *reproduction of the species*, all contained within one small general area called the *Moving-Instinctive Center*.

1. Push the tip of the tongue back against the roof of the mouth.

---

* It is not effective to try to open the solar plexus by concentrating on the forehead or pineal gland. This is a common mistake. It is dangerous and unnecessary to use forced breathing techniques to open the solar plexus.

2. Vocalize Humming Mantra, high-pitched and nasal. Experiment with pitch to find the right vibration which reverberates in the abdomen.
3. Placing the fingers over the abdominal region, exhale — pushing the abdomen in and feeling the reverberation with the hands.
4. Remove the hands and pull the abdomen in by mental command. There should be some effort, but not discomfort.
5. Pull abdomen in at the end of each outbreath. Practice until the reverberation is felt strongly through the whole abdominal region.

GHAAA!

As you sound the Humming Mantra, pronounce "Ghaaa!" and at the same time, pull the abdomen in sharply. Sense the resulting force as it hits each of the Centers. When it reaches the top of the head, turn it downward through the pineal gland and back into the Power Center, arching in front of the body briefly. Begin in a low pitch, then higher, using the three tones — mental, feeling, and power, gradually increasing the speed. Ghaaa! lightly at the first six Centers, then Ghaaa! hard with a rasping sound as you kick the energy back down toward the Power Center. Repeat no more than seven times in one daily exercise session.

SILENT GHAAA!

After completing one full pass of the *Ghaaa Exercise* — striking each Center seven times — close the eyes and silently, without movement, feel the reverberation of the Ghaaa! sound as it continues to create harmonics through the body, particularly in the area of the Adam's Apple and the roof of the mouth.

Continue to do this until you are able to perceive and feel this reverberation instantly. You should be able to create it silently without having to first vocalize it.

ENERGIZING THE BODY CELLS

Energy moves in a spiral form, simultaneously expanding and contracting.

Creative force motivates every form, every manifestation of new life, reproduction of new cells in bodies and the impulse to return to earth in a new form or incarnation.

Control of this energy and storage of it makes it available for use in Objective Sex — Sharing Love Energy — which is the method by which those who use Objective Sex move up the evolutionary ladder into the superconscious state.

1. Sit straight up, eyes closed, hands lightly placed over the abdominal region, just below the navel.
2. Take deep breaths as given in the Deep Breathing Exercise, filling the lower part of the lungs, causing the abdomen to push outward against the hands.
3. Use the Humming Mantra. Feel the resulting reverberation in the abdominal region. This is the purpose of placing the hands over this region.

4. See spirals of *Love Energy* coming into the body, radiating each cell with awakening energy and life force.

ENERGIZING THE SEX CENTER

1. Eyes closed, mask dropped and body relaxed, push *Love Energy* from the Power Center to the Moving-Instinctive Center, at the same time grunting the sound *"Hig!"*
2. Fill the middle lung region with air, centering it just over the heart.
3. Chant the Humming Mantra, feeling the resulting reverberation of the body in the Moving-Instinctive Center. Now you are storing the *Love Energy* in the Moving-Instinctive Center, ready to use.
4. Now push the waves of radiation out of your BodySpace, and see your partner receiving the energy, silently chanting the "Transference Mantra" — *"Ghaaa!"*
5. Feel the *Love Energy* radiating from your BodySpace to the other person's BodySpace.
6. Know that the *Love Energy* was received.

This is intended to be used between consenting partners in Objective Sex. By using this technique one forges a bond between oneself and another.

AWAKENING THE FEELING CENTER
IN ANOTHER

Love is the primary attractive power. When this feeling energy occurs between planets — which are beings of a higher order — it is called "emanation", or "gravity". When it occurs between electronic particles, it is called "atomic attraction", or "radiation", and when between Essences, it is called Objective Love.

Love is a level of vibration unique in the Universe. It acts in pulsing waves of energy, rather than in a continuous stream.

One can feel this energy flowing through the BodySpace and falling into the solar plexus if one knows where to place one's attention.

1. Spread the fingers like a fan. Place the hands over the chest near the heart.
2. Sit straight up, abdomen pulled up and in.
3. Fill the middle lung region, trying to push the chest outward in all directions.
4. Begin the Humming Mantra, "*Humn-Yangm-Ghaaa*", feeling the reverberation in the chest just under the hands.
5. When the reverberation feels right, see yourself as a source of Love Energy, drawing in raw power and transforming it into love energy for the use of other beings.
6. See this energy going out, radiating away from your BodySpace in waves. Direct this energy toward the person in whom you wish to awaken the feeling center. See that person reverbera-

ting with the sound and with your own
vibration.
*Note: This is the key to channelling the force as a
healing agent.*

CREATING THE ETHERIC DOUBLE

There is no other method as powerful and effective
as this. It is strongly advised that one master the
techniques given previously.

Prior to applying this technique, the Humming
Meditation Breathing technique should be used for
ten or fifteen minutes, in order to awaken all centers
and connect the Power Center.

1. Place a blue 25 watt light bulb about six feet
    above the floor.
2. Place a straightback comfortable chair about
    seven or eight feet from the light.
3. Sit in the chair facing the blue bulb, feet flat on
    the floor, elbows resting on the knees.
4. Rest the chin in the cup of the hands.
5. Bend the head backward a little, at the same
    time opening the eyes as much as possible. Do
    not create so much tension that it causes
    discomfort.
6. Look at the light.
7. Remain absolutely still, using the long slow
    breath. Do not blink or move the body muscles
    during this exercise.
8. Do this for only five minutes each day, the first
    week; six minutes per day the second week;
    eight minutes the third week; twelve

minutes the fourth week; fifteen minutes per day the fifth week. After this, one may increase the practice time by one minute per week.

One day as you are doing this exercise the light will vanish completely — not just an optical effect — it will really disappear. When the light disappears, you will be looking through a tube at your own face, as if in a reversed telescope.

The ether has become a mirror for your physical form. You have made an *etheric double*.

When this image replaces the image of the light, you are telepathic.

To communicate telepathically, simply substitute the image of your partner for your own etheric double. Do not try to "talk" or "whisper" communications. Just sense that you are communicating. The simultaneous attention to *Akashic Thoughts* is the real secret of telepathic communion.

After a bit of practice you will discover that you can now be anywhere where ether exists — which is anywhere in the universe. You are able to project your presence there, and see, hear, feel, know, sense and touch things through etheric forms.

In the exterior state you are now able to know what others are thinking and you can use this power to diagnose illness and psychically heal others.

THE METHOD FOR CREATING COMMUNICATION THROUGH TONES

Every effect can be caused by resonance. A basic law of this class of laws is "Like is Equal to Like", or the *Law of Similarity*. Another expression of law within this class of operating factors is "Like Arouses Like". This is the *Law of Contagion*.

You have been given exercises using the Humming Breath which makes possible the vibration of any part of the body through the use of tone.

The human voice is capable of creating *three basic tones*, depending upon the part of the body in which the vibration is intentionally or accidentally reverberated.

When the vibration is reverberated in the head, or in the upper chest without also vibrating the lower part of the chest, a powerful force called the *Mental Tone* is produced. This is useful for indicating data, explaining things, and for arousing a crisper perception in others.

Mental Tone is a denying force. When using a Mental Tone the other person will always resist, especially if it is an instruction or a command.

In presenting data, the Mental Tone is used, thus creating a reverberation *in the mind* of the individual to whom you are communicating mental concepts.

Feelings should always be expressed and conveyed through the *Feeling Tone*. It should always be used when conveying remorse, compassion, results of conscience, or sincerity.

Use the Feeling Tone for elimination of friction between yourself and others. The Feeling Tone can only be produced if the full chest, *including the lower back part*, is set into motion, creating overtones and harmonics.

Exercise:

1. Fill the upper part of the chest with air. Make the tone reverberate in the lower chest, at the same time wishing to express compassion, conscience, and sincerity. It is important to be authentic when doing this. It is impossible to create real moods when one really feels another way.

2. Placing the hands over the heart, speak softly, lowering the voice until you can feel the rumbling vibration of your tone in the heart. As you speak, put your attention on the tone. Control it constantly in this way. In this tone, you can say anything to anyone and they will not be annoyed or angry with you. Additionally, *you cannot be annoyed at anyone else* when you are using this tone of Love.

3. The *Power Tone* is always supported through the action of the large abdominal muscles. Using these muscles to support vocalization puts power and feeling into an expression, thus creating an instant effect on the environment.

4. With every phrase, see it landing as a blow to the chest, but in a kind and gentle way, as if sparring with a friend. Grow into the habit of using this decisive and impelling power in your tone. Keep your voice gentle and low-pitched. When using this tone, never allow your voice

to become demanding or like a sergeant's drill tone. *Gentleness is the key.*

5. Also when using the Power Tone it is vital that one remain in a state of beneficence and compassion toward others, using this tone and its accompanying authority only for the good of others. It is a Tone reserved for work toward Conscious Aims, such as instructions from coaches or a Teacher, or for communication during Objective Sex or similar exercises — as the command to *withdraw* or to vibrate the *Humming* and other Mantras.

THE THREE TONES OF COMMUNICATION:

Developing the Mental Tone:

1. Take a very short breath into the top of the chest.
2. Keeping the tone confined to the head, sound the Humming Mantra, allowing it to reverberate only in the head.
3. Note that there is no vibration in the chest.
4. When using the Humming Mantra for this exercise, it should be vocalized as *"Humn-Yangm-Ghaaa"*, in a high-pitched nasal tone.
5. Now try altering the pitch while retaining the Mental Tone.
6. Try using this tone to give a command.

Developing the Feeling Tone:

1. Take a deep breath to fill the upper chest.
2. Place the hands over the heart area.
3. Feel the wish to express compassion and love.
4. Chant the mantra *"Humn-Yangm-Ghaaa"*, pitching the voice about medium range.
5. Continue practicing this until you can sense the reverberation strongly in the heart region. You will notice that this feeling gets stronger as you practice each day.

Developing the Power Tone:

1. Filling the chest full of air in the deep breathing technique, feel the expansion of air into the sympathetic nervous system as the air is expressed outward during speech.
2. Place the hand over the abdomen.
3. Feel the decision to state something, and your certainty about what you are about to say.
4. Chant the mantra *"Humn-Yangm-Ghaaa"*, keeping the tone low-pitched.
5. Continue practicing this until you can definitely sense the reverberation in the abdomen. Be sure to remember to contract the abdominal muscles forcefully as you vocally express sound in the Power Tone.

You will find many people in life who fail because they use the *Mental Tone* when dealing with others.

By simply altering the tone, lowering the pitch, and reverberating the sound in the correct center, one can develop great success in dealing with, and relating to, others.

TANTRIC KEGEL EXERCISE

This exercise is superior for improving the elasticity of the genital muscles and at the same time putting them under voluntary control. You can do this exercise in any position, anywhere. This exercise is excellent for the male partner as well, because it not only massages the prostate gland but increases the control of the sexual energies.

This ancient tantric exercise strengthens the pubococcygeus muscle which passes from the pubic bone at the front of the pelvis box to the coccyx, or tailbone, in the back. The muscle operates in the same way as a circular valve, and is the same muscle that opens and closes the three apertures in the lower torso. These apertures can't be controlled separately by independent muscles, but you *can* exercise to the degree that you can focus the main effort on only one of the openings. Just as with any other muscle of the body that is not completely involuntary, you can gain voluntary control and make it more flexible by daily exercise.

In many cultures the Kegel exercise is used by the female partner to stimulate vaginal orgasm, and to develop a woman's ability to heighten sexual pleasure for her partner.

1. During urination contract the muscles to stop the flow.
2. Observe the muscles used.

3. Hold the muscle in contraction for a second or two, and then release.
4. Do it again.

Once the muscle is located, control of urination has served its purpose. Practice contractions daily in rounds of 75 short (one second) and 75 long (three seconds). For additional instructions see **Sexual Energy Ecstasy** by Ramsdale and Dorfman.

BREAKING THROUGH

Even though at first you will be using the Humming Mantra and some movement of the Kegel muscle, stillness and silence become important later on.

Light does not experience vibration, nor does it experience sound or perception of movement. This is an important point, because you are trying through these exercises to achieve the speed of light — which is stillness and silence.

The major points to remember are: *Stillness, Attention, Communication,* and *Silence,* or *SACS.*

As you work with each other, you will find that relaxation of the body muscles becomes easier, and as the social programming wears off, you will not feel compelled to dramatize pleasure through the use of muscles.

Tension of the abdominal and stomach muscles can easily cause orgasm or create a buildup of body vibration due to excitement. It is important to fully relax — especially the abdominal, stomach, genital, anus, and lower back muscles.

These are all mentally connected to the facial muscles. If you remember to relax the face mask it will help you to remember to also relax the abdominal and lower back muscles.

In order to move out of BodySpace into other higher spaces it will be necessary at first to use the Meditation and Visualizing exercises, given in "Journey through the Great Mother".* Later, this will not be necessary, and you may even prefer to dispense with them in the beginning, just using them to familiarize yourself with the spaces and visualizations in their natural sequence. You can read them together, discuss any spaces that you have gotten into, and then begin contact.

You will find that certain spaces have obstacles at the entrance, and that you will have to use a mantra in order to break through these barriers and move into the new space.

The Humming Mantra can be used silently. *Never use the Humming Mantra vocally when in the Expanded State of MetaSpace.*

In MetaSpace, the slightest movement can cause unwanted reverberations. The attitude of reverence and respect for these spaces is important. In some spaces there are Guides who will offer instruction on what to do, and may offer knowledge which you can use for your own Essence development.

Listen, be aware, be there with attention, remain in communication with your partner; *be alive.*

*A tape is available to guide you (see page 185). If this visualization exercise feels artificial, you may start with other techniques in the book that move you out of BodySpace, e.g., the Humming Mantra.

ENDURANCE

The tantric effect doesn't begin to occur until an hour or more after beginning sexual contact. You will have to go beyond the first few barriers in order to arrive at the state in which Objective Sex is possible.

The *first point of climax* will usually occur about two or three minutes after first contact. Most men can easily bypass this by slowing the movement, by becoming still, or by withdrawing for a few moments.

The *second point of climax* usually occurs after about five or ten minutes, and unless bypassed will result in a short emission of semen. It is easy to bypass this through use of relaxation and if necessary temporary withdrawal.

The *third point of climax* is reached just before the time one would ordinarily complete sexual contact. One can usually tell when this is approaching — according to previous sexual encounters — and can simply slow the movement, stop, or withdraw. It is best to do this for a sufficient period to allow the entire crescendo to die down — and even better to simply withdraw about ten minutes before climax would occur, and wait about twenty minutes before resuming contact, or until the body is completely calm.

In this first series of stages, it is best to just have sexual contact and movement in the ordinary way. But *once the third point of climax has been bypassed* it will be easy to continue without movement or erotic sensation.

The penis can be made to move because there are muscles which can manipulate it. These muscles can be strengthened using the Kegel technique.

Ordinarily the penis is not controlled voluntarily. But control of erection and penile movement can be transferred from the involuntary brain to the voluntary brain simply by daily practice at the Kegel exercise. It is quite easy to accomplish this transference.

Dependence upon erotic mental pictures to arouse penile erection keeps the penile muscles under involuntary control, so it is best to work at going beyond erotic mental picture stimulation.

Erections occur in cycles. Men will find that sometimes they have a full erection and sometimes they don't. This should not be cause for concern. Allow the erection mechanism to work with this cycle, unless it becomes necessary to arouse an erection in order to maintain sexual contact. In this case, the Kegel muscle should be contracted rapidly, but without other movement, until the erection is regained. After a while it will not even be necessary to do this. Just by *willing* it to be so, the penis can be caused to have an erection. It may take daily practice for several months before this can be attained.

Breathing correctly is also important in going beyond climax, and in maintaining penile erection. It controls the body's natural tendency to become excited, and quiets the mind.

In the first few minutes of sexual contact, excitement is quite high, because the reproductive urge contained in the Moving Center becomes active, trying to achieve climax as quickly as possible. This is simply a survival mechanism, and can easily be bypassed.

At the *second point of climax* the shock of contact with the nerve endings and its resulting impact on the nervous system causes the impulse to climax once again. This is a protective mechanism in the nervous system to prevent shock, high activity, and over-stimulation. Again, this can be bypassed.

The *third point of climax* is a result of the psyche's resistance to effort. Once coitus has been achieved, the psyche wishes to relieve the muscle tension and stress and regain equilibrium. Just by realizing that effort is required, one can bypass this barrier. The impulse to have an orgasm at this point can be quite overwhelming, especially if one is in the habit of allowing the orgasm to come "as a surprise". With a little practice this can be handled quite easily.

Do not become discouraged if it takes a few sessions before even a small gain in willpower is accomplished. You are overcoming body programs and survival mechanisms — and they are very powerful.

By persevering one can win control of these simple muscle and nervous system factors. It is perseverence that counts.

One makes the same type of effort at re-training the genitals and climax impulses as one would make in training a dog. The point is to *never let the dog win*. If the dog wins even once, it becomes impossible afterward to train it to do what you want it to do. At the same time, it must be rewarded with harmless treats for its efforts.

In sexual re-training, it is important to try these exercises on a gently increasing sequence of difficulty. Never go beyond your ability at the moment or you may lose the initiative.

BYPASSING ORGASM

The best way to use breathing to overcome the impulse of climax is to begin deep breathing at the first moment you realize the impulse is building. As you become more and more conscious of this impulse and its accompanying sensations, you will recognize it sooner. Tuning in to the subtle variations of the nervous system, body, and psyche in this way is a necessary sensing skill in achieving and maintaining the Objective Sex state.

One cannot be careless or allow climax to surprise one through laziness or inattentiveness. One must make the effort to control the natural and automatic impulses to climax which occur periodically in the beginning of sexual contact, and at intervals of about one or two hours thereafter, should one continue contact beyond the first hour.

It is best to build up slowly to longer periods of contact, beginning with only one hour and gradually increasing contact time by ten or fifteen minutes each day. In this way sessions of contact can be increased easily to periods of several hours in only a few weeks or a month.

The impulse to climax is called "momentum", which simply means *wanting to continue the same action*. There is momentum of the body and momentum of the psyche. Each of these impulses must be overcome by effort and willpower. Therefore it is important to make an affirmation before sexual contact. This affirmation simply means that both partners intend to accomplish something specific. *It is an agreement not to succumb to the impulse to climax.*

Once the first half hour or so of climactic impulses have been bypassed, it is possible to continue sexual contact almost indefinitely. The penis can remain erect naturally for several hours after the first hour of contact. The nerve endings have been so over-stimulated that they do not cause release of tension.

The important thing about continuing past the first hour is relaxation of the body. At the same time, one should not allow lethargy to set in. This can be avoided by keeping oneself mentally alert and interested, without expecting results of any specific kind — and at the same time allowing the body to relax fully.

At about the one hour mark, one will find that the Expanded State is being entered without effort or direction. This natural entry into *MetaSpace* occurs just because the nervous system has been so overstimulated that it cannot hold the *BodySpace* state any longer.

As you experiment with this, you will discover that the slightest movement will bring you back out of *MetaSpace* into *BodySpace*, at least momentarily. This breaks the contact somewhat, and should be avoided except for purposes of early experimentation with these Spaces.

There are no rules about these spaces except to be gentle and compassionate, and to avoid excitement and violence, especially the violence of desire or upset. If you become upset for any reason, you will find that *MetaSpace* naturally rejects your presence, returning you instantly to *BodySpace*, where it is permitted to be aggressive, violent or passionate.

If *MetaSpace* can be characterized, it can be said to be non-passionate. If you have been dependent upon passion and erotic sensation to be able to continue sexual contact, it will be a new learning situation for you to have sex in a different way.

The Beginning Exercises are excellent methods to build this new approach to sexual contact. After a while it will become so natural to bypass orgasm that no physical stoppage or withdrawal is necessary. You will be surprised how quickly will-power builds in this regard once the decision is made to accomplish this, and the integrity of the decision is realized.

DEBRIEFING ROUTINE

1. Sponge bath.
2. Deep breathing exercises.
3. Sit up 45° until breath recovery is normal.
4. Stand and extend arms upward, sideways, forward.
5. Sit on knees for a few moments.
6. Place hands back of neck and breathe slowly to relieve any spinal pressure.
7. Take a hot herbal bath or a shower. We use showers in the workshops.
8. Lie down and review the entire experience with partner.
9. Together, write a report of the entire experience that occurred during the exercise. (Refer to Objective Sex Workshop Student Reports.)

JOURNEY
THROUGH
THE
GREAT
MOTHER

THE DANCE

Each manifestation of the Great Mother has her own Tantra, or Path, her own Mantra, or sound, and her own Yantra, or visualization.

She is the bridge over which one can cross into the Great Void, but she must be followed according to her own special ritual.

One receives the ritual of each of the Devis, or goddesses, by serving her and by learning her ways.

The explorer of the Great Mother is the male. Without him, she could not become known. He entertains her with his antics and she watches his progress with interest, for he can do things that are not possible for her. He can suffer, he can imagine himself confronted with great obstacles, he can be betrayed, he can love, he can die.

Life is for him an appreciation of her. And through his life she appreciates herself.

And between them somehow eternity is made just a little more bearable. The stark reality of formlessness and endlessness has been conquered.

In the space just outside the universe stand two Guides, the Guide of Light and the Guide of Darkness. They stand to the right and to the left of the entrance to the Great Mother. With them and standing between them is the Guide of

the Upward Path. With
Her, they form the Sun,
the Moon, and the Dark-
ness of Space.

ithin the entrance is
the luminous spider-
web of existence. She
contains within Her form
all life, action and thought.
Upon Her rests the nour-
ishment of life. Within
Her there is only the
hollow emptiness of the
Void. But in the Void She
manifests all forms.

Her body forms the chain from the womb to the tomb. Her power extends from the phallus within Her to the Secret House of the Void, in which the Essence dwells eternally.

In the depths of Her entrance stands the Sixfold Guide, shining with the light of the Six Worlds. She is the manifestation of the Mantra of Six Syllables.

She appears within the quiet presence of a mirror of light, shining as a silk thread strung with diamonds. She is the Holder of the Knowledge of Sound. Through Her one can travel the Great Path which leads to the Spaceless and Timeless Void before Creation, the Primordial Being.

She is the Subtle A-wakener, whose real nature is that of the Shining Void. She is the mixer of the annointing oils of white and red which flow downward from the Source of all Nectars.

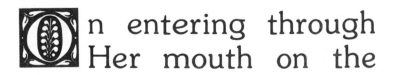he Pillars of Wisdom can be seen within Her open mouth, which is filled with the Nectar of Fire. She is the Guide of the Place of Union, the Endless Knot leading to the Center of the Void which has no center.

On entering through Her mouth on the

Upward Path, one comes to the Red Room of the Rosy Cross. Above one there is an opening in the ceiling. It reveals an open mouth that shines golden in the dull red light of this room.

This is the channel by which one can travel to the Highest Space of the Void, the Place of the Guide, within which one becomes the Guide, for there is no one else in the Center of the Void.

It is here that one is able to make the Unspeakable Sacrifice of Holder of Eternal Knowledge and Creator of Infinity.

One can see the mouth of this channel opening downward. On its surface one can read the four letters of the Secret Mantra which opens this door. By illuminating this Mantra with the Power of Meditation contained in the Humming Breath (see

Intermediate   Exercises)
this Mantra can be read.
Repeating   this   Mantra
opens the door upward,
and one is now able to
pass into the Inner Chamber of the next room.

ere one encounters
the King of Creators, the Child of Creation seated upon His lap.
Near   them   stands   the
Keeper of the Second
Door, Her arms luminous
white, Her eyes shining
with the deep red color of
rubies.

She holds the Key to Divine Knowledge and Direct Revelation. She strikes terror into the hearts of the unprepared, for She is also the Holder of the Key of Immortality beyond the limits of the universe and behind the veil, the apparent reality of the created world.

Next to Her, within the wall of the room, there shines the soft luminous triangle form of an open doorway, nestled in the deep redness of the Living, Throbbing surface. Within this open mouth is the opening and closing sphincter of the Guardian of the Third Room. It pulses in rhythmic beating as if to the thrumming of a Great Heart.

It will open when the words of the Secret Mantra surrounding the opening have been illuminated by the Power of Meditation and repeated.

Past this entrance is the Room of the Guide of Higher Form, the Room of the Garnet. Here one takes in the atmosphere of the Higher Cosmos, and after transforming it during the pause between breaths, it is released along the Luminous Network of the Higher Body at the same time the exhaling breath is released. As the inhaling breath, or "Haam" is taken, the Higher Atmosphere particles are ab-

sorbed. And as the ex-
haling breath, or ''Saah''
is released, it is broken
into smaller particles cor-
responding to the lower
world and sent to energize
the Higher Body being
born there.

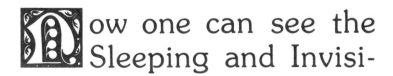 s one moves through
this region, one can
feel the swirling of the
Three Forces as they mix
together.

ow one can see the
Sleeping and Invisi-

ble Form of the Serpent, the Weaver of Dreams, coiled around the mouth of the entrance to the next room. She is the Creator of the Web of Life. She gently and softly covers the entrance to the next room with Her body, and unless one is careful it is possible to accidentally enter Her Coils of Illusion rather than proceed upward toward the Center of the Void. One may even imagine that one has succeeded in passing Her,

should one become im-
mersed in Her Dreams.

ithin the mound
formed by Her body
is the opening through
which one must now travel
to get into the next room.
Her Coils can be opened
and passed by repeating
the Mantra inscribed on
Her body. This Mantra
can be illuminated by the
Power of Meditation, and
once seen it must be
repeated immediately, for
its Power diminishes with-

in moments after it has been revealed.

One travels through the entrance past a blue-green phallic form, rolled in the shape of a rosebud, tapered toward the opening. Its aperture is at the bottom. One must go through this opening to get into the next room.

In the next room, the Blue-Green Room of the Opal, a light emanates from the opening of the next gateway. The blue-green light emits no heat, and the atmosphere is cool and pleasant to one's sensations. Here communication is only possible by gesture. The dark, cool light of the room suggests sleep, but one must not succumb to this urge.

In this space one has access to the Secret of the Essence and to the Knowledge of Conscious Conception of a child....

This is the space of the Higher Forms of Rebirth.

ere one will be given the Throbbing Bone and the Crystal Sphere. Within the Throbbing Bone is the Secret of Life, if it can be read. And within the Sphere is the whole content of Space and Time, accessible through absorption.

n this space one is free from the pain and suffering of the world.

One will be taken from the form of an armed and legged creature to the perfect form of the Crystal Sphere. One is taken now by the Guide of the Universe, through whom the world is provided with Light. It is Her Nectar that flows into the world, illuminating the Crucible of Reality.

ere one may move into side dimensions and alternate realities. Now one moves past this

Guardian who glistens with self radiance and whose form shimmers with chain-lightning. One can hear Her sound — that of a swarm of humming bees — diminish as one moves into the next room.

ow one is in the Blue Room of the Star Sapphire. At the sides one can see the swirling forms of the waiting Guides, of which there are three. Here one encounters the Old One, white-haired and dressed in shabby garments. He offers one the understanding of Life and of Love. To learn from Him, one must go beyond the appearance of form.

here one encounters the Dark Lady, who wears upon Her hand the Ring of Garnets.

here one is safe from all harm and from the tendencies of lust, anger, jealousy, greed, hatred and fear. If one is not able to release oneself from these habits, one cannot enter this room and is rejected by the Guardian at the door.

In this space one is freed from the bondage of sleep and ignorance of limited consciousness. By transcending these one is able to continue on the Upward Path. One is now able to hear the Teaching without translating it into the language of the mind.

bove and past this is the White Room of the Clouds of Unknowing. Here one encounters the Guide of Form and Perception. He removes the remains of karma which may still cling to one without one being aware of their presence.

ehind one now one will see the door to the next chamber. It can only be opened by repeating the Secret Mantra written above it on the lintel of the door. This Mantra also must be illuminated by the Power of Meditation in order to be visible.

In the next chamber one encounters the Guide of the Six-Cornered Room. The atmosphere here is a smoky blue-gray. One can feel but not hear a rhythmic pulsing drumming. One may also feel a periodic expansion and contraction of the walls, slight, but visible to the attentive.

This is the space of the Guide of the Soundless Sound in the realm of No Vibration. Here one is taken beyond one's own limits of expansion into attainments unknowable by ordinary consciousness.

As one passes through this space the atmosphere will make orientation difficult. One must trust the Guides to help one through to the next chamber. One will be almost overwhelmed by the sweet smell of the heavy blue-gray smoke. There seems to be no way out, but through a change in consciousness and vibration level one will eventually see the way to the next chamber.

The door is opened in the same way as the others, by illuminating the

Mantra above the door through the Power of Meditation.

Now one finds oneself in the Vermilion Room of the Star ruby. Here one encounters the form of the Little Mother, happily enjoying this reality as one enjoys a bubble-bath. She is compassionate and can be helpful in attaining one's aim to go on to higher spaces.

pon Her form one can see a tiny golden shape, a soft triangle. Within this form one will notice an opening as small as a pinhole. It is through this opening that one must pass, and one must depend upon Her for help in this. Behind Her there are several doors, but these all lead downward. They are the Doors to Dreams and Illusion. Only through the opening on Her form is it possible to move upward. Ask Her and She

will give the Secret of
Passing Her Doors.

In the next room one
is given the Knowledge of Cosmic Maintenance and the means for
helping other forms of life
attain consciousness.
Here the exhalation of the
atmosphere from Higher
Cosmoses passes downward into the Void to
become material for new
forms of Creation.

One can see the filaments projecting from the opening in this doorway into the surrounding area of Her flesh, as one passes through the tiny aperture into the next chamber.

Here one uses the Mantra "Ma-Ma", concentrating meanwhile on the Guide who holds in His ten fingers the form of creation for all worlds.

One meets here the Guide who is beloved of all women, whose senses and actions are in control of the Essence of the Void, and whose thoughts and feelings are those proper only to Essence. His speech flows like golden honey.

He is the Guide of the Path of Liberation. Through Him one is able to master the Power of entering and leaving any physical form, even though occupied by another being. Through Him one learns the Secret of

Invisibility and Sky-Walking and the Secret of Forms as Holders of Identity.

Now one sees yet another doorway, over which is inscribed the Secret Mantra of the Guardian of the Violet Room of the Sacred Nectar. In this space the unformed substance of the universe is stored until it is given form and solidity.

In the outer rim of this chamber is the Edge of the Void, through which passes pure energy to become matter as it enters the universe contained in the Crystal Sphere. This is the room of the Diaphragm of Space.

Upon a gray mound on the wall one can see a snowy white form, at the top of which is a small aperture. Upon this gray mound one who is able to illuminate through the Power of Meditation will see a Mantra emblazoned on its surface, the letters rippling with light like chain-lightning. Repeating this Mantra will open the gateway, allowing one to proceed in the Upward Path.

Now one finds oneself in the Yellow Room of the Diamond. In this space one encounters the Source of Nectar, the Ocean of Ambrosia, the Liquid Fire which is stored here before pouring over the Edge of the Void into the streams and channels which form the network of life within the Great Mother.

Surrounding one now are many doors, only one of which is the real gateway to the Inner Chamber. Only one who has attained purity is able to choose between them.

One who has awakened to the complete knowledge of Essence will now awaken to the state of Perfected Reason while in this space.

One should now concentrate one's full attention on maintaining an uninterrupted state of reverie, not allowing the attention to wander or to fall upon distractions, as one searches for the right gateway.

One sees here everything which has occurred in the past, pres-

ent and future of the world
of form, and one is the
Liberator of Beings of all
forms during the time one
remains in this space.

ow one stands at the
very Brink of End-
lessness. With one's
attention firmly rooted to
the form of the Guide of
the Diamond Room, and
controlling one's breath
with the Humming Man-
tra, one is able to move
toward the center of the
door which now stands

open.

One should move past this, and if one has chosen correctly, one should now be standing within the Room of the Clear Light, from which all thought issues into Reality. Here one can see yet another Mantra emblazoned on a mound in the center of the room. It can only be illuminated by the Power of Meditation, and when one focuses this Power on the mound, the entire room is brilliantly lighted by Clear White Light.

Now one is able to see the Guide of the Book of Knowledge. She is the formless mind, pure white Essence, the Holder of the Key of Uncreation and Supreme Understanding.

Within this room only the Body of Habits can exist. Here one must function without the mind.

One can look down at oneself now and should one see no form or only a partial form, one has not yet crystallized one's Higher Being Body.

Within the form of the Guide of the Book of Knowledge one can see a vibrating and glowing phallic form running the length of Her body. It is crystalline white with ripples of purple flashing over its surface like chain-lightning. Upon this

Primary Form of the Guide of the Book of Knowledge are the letters of the Primordial Mantra, which can only be seen when illuminated by the Power of Meditation.

Through recognition of this gateway one can move into the space beyond, in which one becomes the Ever-Living Guide, the maintainer of all forms of existence, and Guide to Liberation for all Beings everywhere.

By repeating the Mantra thus revealed, one moves through the gateway into the chamber within.

As one moves more deeply into this space one is able to discern the letters of the Mantra which forms the Sacred Verses of the Innermost Sphere of Reality, the Center of the Void.

ne is now within the Flame Which Does

Not Burn, forming with one's own Essence the Light of the Universe. Above one is a crescent moon, which is the Form of the Mantra of Nothingness.

When one releases connection with the worlds below, realization of Endlessness is attained. One forms the Closing of Essence by placing the left heel against the anus, right heel over left, and with the lips formed into a flute embouchure one slowly draws the inbreath, thus filling the lower belly with air. At the same time, one closes the ears with the thumbs, the eyes with the forefingers, the nostrils with the middle fingers, and the mouth with the remaining fingers.

Now one exhales slowly, using the Deep Breathing Technique, and with the perceptions and sensing kept at a steady rate, one enters Deep Essence Reverie while focusing on the Humming Mantra.

hen one has mastered this Closing of the Essence and has attained the Knowledge of Form and Space which can only be transmitted in this space, and one has obtained Knowledge through Service to the Guide, one is able to perceive now the soft triangular form of the next gateway. Upon this mound one will perceive the Mantra which will allow one to move through it, upward into the next higher Chamber.

To one who has practiced the Visualizing Exercises the visions of the Inner Sphere become visible.

It is in this room that the Guide manifests Himself in His full Glory, uncovered and unshrouded, as the source of All.

He is forever beyond the effects of time and space, and every existing created object is within His sight. Here the walls form the outermost limits of infinity, and yet they seem only a few feet away.

In this room everything passes away in the dissolving radiations of Grace.

The Father/Mother is manifested in deep Union as the form of MA, surrounded by the form of the created world, the form of MA-YA. Here dwells the Eternal Being, in the form of a single grain whose double-form-ed germ is covered by an outer sheath of skin. It remains motionless and yet all forms of Reality are emanated from this single grain, the Mustard Seed of Creation.

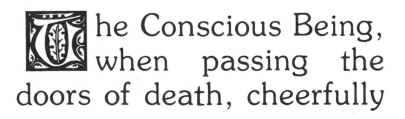he Conscious Being, when passing the doors of death, cheerfully

places his breath into this space, and after having passed the doors of death enters into this Endless and Primordial state which existed before the world was created and after the world was destroyed.

When one has perfected one's relationship with the Guide through Service, one will see above this chamber the form of the Intermediate Causal Body. Through the Power of Meditation one can illuminate the Mantra necessary to open this gateway.

This entrance, which is the space in which formlessness and endlessness are dissolved, is shaped in the form of a crescent moon, bent to form a plowshare.

Above this is the space of the Void in which the Supreme Ether remains forever unmanifested and unformed.

This room, white, lustrous and self-luminous as the full moon, has within it the Guide of Sleep and Dreaming. In order to remain awake here one must immediately apply the Mantra given by the Guide during one's service period in the world.

Surrounding this form of the Guide are filaments in clusters, colored like the early morning sun. In the deep meditation of Essence one can clearly see the letters written on its surface, and by uttering this Mantra one becomes one with the Guide of Sleep and Dreaming, thus passing this barrier and revealing the Path to the Secret Room of the Guide.

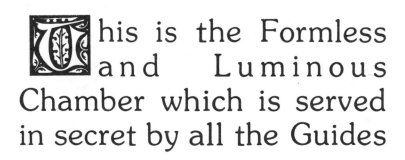his is the Formless and Luminous Chamber which is served in secret by all the Guides

and by all true Seekers. Here one learns the secret methods for ingestion of food, evacuation of waste, and for Conscious Sex.

Now one discovers the Concealed Chamber which is only attainable by Great Effort. This is the Chamber from which the Nectar of Essence originates, and in which the Root of all Awakening and Liberation is found.

One encounters here the Guide of Emanations and Radiations, who dissolves all Manifestation. Through His emanations and radiations a continuous stream of Nectar is formed from the Primordial Mantra, the One Word.

Now one is instructed by the Guide in Knowledge in which the realization of the unity of Psyche and Essence is understood.

The Guide pervades all things in which He and He Alone is immanent, as all things are formed from Him. He is the cause of the vivifying current which flows through all living things by the power of inbreath and outbreath. He is the silence between breaths, and His name is the Mantra of HaamSaah.

The Creator calls this the Place of Creation. The Maintainer calls

it the Home of the Gods. The Destroyer calls it the Place of Union. Saints call it the Place of Compassion, and Angels call it the Throne of God. It is the Place in which the Three become Two, and the Two become One.

The Guide of the Moon dwells here, colored like the morning sun, fine as the silken thread of the spider's web, soft and radiant as a cloud. It is She who maintains the forms of all those who have bodies.

Inside this chamber is the Guide of the Nirvanic Worlds. She is as subtle as the breadth of a hair, as silent as the windless night. She is the Ever-Present Guide of the Inner World, the Unknowable which is within all beings.

She is the Holder of Divine Knowledge Beyond All Knowledge, and is formed from the Light of all Radiations and Emanations from all worlds. She is the Voidness which remains when all Twelve Suns of the Samsaric and Nirvanic Worlds appear in the same space at the same time.

Within Her, in the midst of Her shockingly stunning form, is the Primordial Matrix of Nirvana. She is the Guide who provides the Place of Liberation for all Beings who tire of the created worlds. She is the Mother of Buddhas and the Protector of Saints and Messengers, the Home of Prophets and the Refuge of Total Freedom.

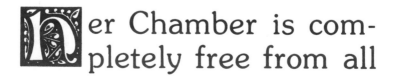he graciously holds the Knowledge of Truth for all Liberated Beings until they are ready to Awaken.

Her Chamber is completely free from all

illusions of form and of mind, and is attainable only by Beings who have mastered the Self and conquered the Body of Habits. Her name is known only as the Ineffable Essence of Nothing.

One who has purified oneself of all unconscious habits through the practice of meditation and action is now able to learn directly from the Guide through transmission the exact Method of the Great Awakening.

One should now immerse one's whole Being in the Mantra of Receiving Teaching (only given orally from Teacher to Pupil through Initiation) and piercing the center of the invisible aperture of the Mouth Which Never Opens, one moves through this into the chamber beyond, closing the door behind one, through the Power of the Breath of Fire (not given here, as breath-coaching is necessary for mastery and safety. An alternative is given on page 174 for students who do not have a breath-coach or will not seek the help of a Teacher.)

Both partners simultaneously experience the resulting piercing of the gateway, and they come to rest in the Great Chamber of the Living Father, in His Eternal State of Formless Being.

When one arrives in this space one should

intentionally allow all forms to be absorbed into the Female form. One thus realizes the identity of the Essence, becoming fully conscious of the Primordial state.

One has come to the abode of the Father, who is the husband of the Great Mother and Father to the Children of the Void. Therefore one is one with Him and at the same moment one finds oneself outside Her, and yet absorbed by Her, neither one nor the other and yet both.

One is now at the End of the Journey and yet it is the beginning of the Journey, for one stands once again at the entrance to Her Womb. Each has dissolved into its Primordial Cause, leaving nothing other than that which is.

One now sees Her as a thousand-headed Serpent, upon whose coils

one sits alone, surrounded
by the Void, and trembling
with the knowledge of
Absolute Reality. But with
one is the Daughter of the
Mother, and through Her
one is calmed and the
Screaming Void is si-
lenced.

Here one may con-
verse with the Per-
fect Lover, the Primordial
Co-Creator. Here one may
share with the Companion
the Everlasting Burden of
Endlessness.

nd when one tires of this, one may once again dance at the feet of the Great Mother and make the Journey through Her, tasting of Her secrets and reveling in the joys and suffering within Her formless form. And She will dance for you, and you shall see Him dance, and the Two shall become many, and the many shall become Three, and the Three shall be Companions for evermore.

ALTERNATIVE BREATH EXERCISE

One sits cross-legged, foreheads pressed together.

Steady the attention through the use of the Humming Mantra and slow breathing technique.

Fill the chest with air all the way down to the lower lungs. Stop the outward flow of air when the lungs have been filled.

Contract the floor of the pelvic muscle (Kegel Muscle) to stop the downward flow of air.

Raising the air upward toward the throat, the male partner suddenly pierces the mouth of the female partner with this breath, releasing it into her lungs for a moment. It is important that this be gentle even though sudden, to avoid physical shock or damage. Use of this exercise with a breath-coach is strongly recommended.

APPENDIX   A

1.0:1.13:1.25:1.33:1.50:1.67:1.88:2.0

RELATIVE RATES OF VIBRATION OF NEW BODY FORMATION:

Body Formation:	Rate of Vibration:
Planetary BodySpace	384.0
Second Body	433.9
Third Body	480.0
Fourth Body	510.7
Fifth Body	576.0
Sixth Body	641.3
Seventh Body	721.9
New Universe	768.0

SCALE OF CONSCIOUSNESS IN RELATION TO BODYSPACE:

1. Stable in the Expanded State.
2. Transference through the Void.
3. Release from BodySpace desires, problems and beliefs.
4. Freedom to move outside BodySpace.
5. Able to cause action in BodySpace from outside it.
6. Able to knowingly choose one's form or identity in BodySpace.
7. Able to view the entire History of Creation from Primordial to the Void, through time to the Omnipresent.
8. Able to determine the consequences of any action in BodySpace.
9. Able to move in and out of BodySpace without negative sensation.
10. Able to be in silent communication.
11. Able to comprehend truth.
12. Able to accept and use the help of the Guides.
13. Able to place oneself anywhere within the Scale of Existence.
14. Able to instantly be anywhere in BodySpace.
15. Able to regulate action in BodySpace to avoid aggression and violence of others.
16. Able to alter one's state of consciousness easily.
17. Able to be outside BodySpace.
18. Not able to be outside BodySpace.
19. Subject to the beliefs of psyche programming.
20. Can't see beyond BodySpace.
21. Stuck in BodySpace.

SCALE OF DEGENERATION INTO BODYSPACE

MetaSpace: Here I am in perfect and total communication with myself. There is no other. There is no frame of reference to frame. Knowing is knowing. All realities and lifetimes are dreams within me. I am my own karma. Why is this always such a big surprise?

MacroSpace: I am able to expand my Knowing even to the state of Not Knowing. This concept has potential.

MonoSpace: Is there another Knower? If there is another Knower, does that Knower Know what this Knower Knows?

SynchroSpace: I am able to create as an expression of Knowing. Maybe there are other Knowers who are willing to express their Knowing in the same way.

SuperSpace: This is how it got out of control. I don't have any idea how it got out of control. I must keep remembering that I don't know how it got out of control.

RevoSpace: Every time I create a space it keeps disappearing. I have to create them again and again to make them continue to exist.

AlterSpace: Creations can't remain the same if I want them to persist. The same creation can only exist in one moment. So I have to change it slightly to get it to exist through time.

ProtoSpace: Changing my creations in order to make them continue to exist means that they have to be different in each moment so I can get a chain of time for my spaces. My creations are degenerating as they get farther away from the Original Creation. My spaces are ageing moment by moment.

SimulSpace: I can forget when I get inside a mass. I wonder what it would be like to be inside that body over there.

OscilloSpace: I wonder if those other Knowers out there are really other Knowers. Did I create other Knowers just to have someone to be out there?

TransSpace: I can forget much better when I can feel it. I'm glad I thought of that.

ParaSpace: I must regain control of all this. But I've forgotten how I did it.

UniSpace: What would be better? To be absolutely safe here, or to plunge down into BodySpace and be subject to accident, death, and pain? I don't want to get hurt, but on the other hand, this is too much.

InfraSpace: I have to resist all these imperfections. All this change is starting to get much too unpredictable.

UltraSpace: I wish I could get rid of all these creations so I could concentrate on how to get back up there. If I could get some peace and quiet I could set it up the way I wanted it to be.

LostinSpace: There has to be a Key to all this Somewhere.

PhiloSpace: I don't want to make another mistake like this. There has to be a new and better way to do this.

PolySpace: Everything has gone wrong. I can't let go.

ContraSpace: I'm trying to like this universe, but look what it did to me.

CoSpace: It's time to withdraw from this thing.

BodySpace: I'll never get out of this alive.

APPENDIX B

INTENTIONAL STRESS FACTORS:

Alterations in Breath Control: *retraining instinctive breathing patterns.* (**Not** *recommended.*)

Artificially Induced Epileptic Seizures: (**Not** *recommended!*)

Artificial Psychosis: *through sleep deprivation, exhaustion, invalidation, irritation, friction, ridicule, and concentration on a chosen reality.*

Attempts at Self-Remembering: *trying to remember to remember oneself.*

Auditory Overload: *bells, organ music, loud sounds.*

Business Problems and Obstacles: *stress of worry.*

Chanting: *enforced repetition of sounds.*

Constant close companionship: *with others who are displeasing or annoying.*

Continual Change: *in the environment and conditions of existence.*

Controlled Dreaming: *directing one's own internal dramas.*
Dance: *under special conditions.*
Death Awareness: *the tombstone at the end of the road.*
Deep Massage: *triggering and releasing images and emotions.*
Delirium: *vacillation between psyche and Essence.*
Dilemma: *trying to resolve apparently paradoxical problems by intense pondering.*
Drugs: *not sopors, but psychedelics, which force attention on overload factors and beliefs — a cop-out for Real Effort.*
Emotional Upsets: *invalidation or ridicule.*
Exposure to a New Culture or Society: *culture shock.*
Failure to Accomplish an Important Goal: *self-dissatisfaction.*
Fasting: *stress induced by focus on the body and overload of the eliminator organs.*
Fervent Prayer: *power-arousal of emotions to peak point, thus causing physical and mental stress.*
Games: *under certain special conditions.*
Gym: *enforced repetition of strenuous exercise of entirely new movements not customary for the body.*
Hypnotism: *controlled and enforced attention and repetition.*
Involuntary Isolation or Imprisonment: *phantasms of isolation.*
Long Periods of Solitude: *enforced confrontation with boredom and the recurring self-programs.*
Mantram: *controlled and enforced attention on repetition of sound and/or significance.*
Meditation: *enforced attention on one single point or enforced confrontation with nothingness.*
Music: *enforced attention on unusual progression of sound and its effect on the organs of the body by resonance.*
Prolonged Artistic Striving: *stress of expression.*
Prolonged Fantasy: *without physical expression or actualization.*
Prolonged Self-Study: *enforced self-discipline of observing the false self without being able to do anything about it.*
Reverie: *deep explorations of the self, which does not exist, the paradox causing severe dilemma of logic and symbolism.*
Religious Ecstasy: *causing body stress and mental stress through overload phenomena.*
Rituals: *enforced repetition of ceremonial actions.*
Running: *body overload.*

Samadhi Tank: *stimulus attenuation and enforced attention on one's internal programming.*
Sex: *arousing the Power Center.*
Shock: *nervous system overload.*
Sustained Danger: *such as primitive existence of paleolithic and neolithic man.*
Theater: *under certain special conditions.*
The Desire for Perfection: *if carried to an extreme.*
The Search for God Within: *The Struggle of Spirit for Redemption.*
Threats to Survival: *stress of fear.*
Trance States: *enforced freeze of the mental flow causing severe stress in the emotional attitudes and physical stress of the organs involved.*
Turning: *sensory and organic stress, combined perceptual paradox.*
Voluntary Periods of Silence: *enforced confrontation with the self and nonaction.*
Yantra: *enforced focus on symbolic forms.*

STRESS HARMFUL TO ESSENCE:

Identification with problems of life.

Suffering from problems of life and relationship.

Pain

Rage

Anger

Fear

Sadness

Paranoia

Panic

Neurotic beliefs

Psychotic insistence on a specific reality.

Migraine

Narcotic withdrawal

Drug states

Orgasm

Masturbation

Daydreaming

Sports

Rock music and dance

Pleasure stimulation

Shock and secondary shock symptoms stemming from physical accident or illness.

Hysteria

Violence

VIBRATIONS:

All spaces are manifested vibrations. This is common knowledge, but there are few practical explanations of how to use this information. To use this, one must realize that a vibration does not occur from only positive or only negative factors. It requires both positive and negative factors, and a Third force which allows them to vibrate in equilibrium. Vibration yes/no.

The positive and negative factors which make up this universe are:

Emotion	*Like/Dislike*
Possessions	*Want/Don't Want*
Desires	Reach/Withdraw
Sensations	*Pleasure/Pain*
Concepts	*Safety/Fear*

In order to get out of BodySpace one must change one's rate of vibration from lower to higher. The combined rate of vibration of the above five factors equals the sound of *AUM*, in middle C. When one alters the basic conflicts of "Yes/No" the resulting vibration creates a new space. One of the primary purposes of the tantric experience is to discover and adopt such higher conflicts.

Higher Conflicts:

Angel — light, goodness/Devil — darkness, the demon within
To Exist/To Cease Existing
Karma/Liberation
Male/Female
Thinking/Reverie
Psyche/Essence
Action/Stillness
BodySpace/MetaSpace
Power/Vulnerability
Knowledge/Foolishness
Communication/Silence
Relationships/Being Alone
Eating/Fasting
Sleep/Exhaustion
Ordinary Efforts/Great Efforts
Conforming/Not Conforming
Emotional Suffering/Conscious Suffering
Loss/Sacrifice
Receiving/Teaching
Learning/Understanding
Discuss the Work/Do the Work
Personal Satisfaction/Pay Back For One's Existence
Gratification/Conscious Life
Motion/No Motion

As you can see, these are not arbitrary conflicts, given in a moral motivation or for social benefit. They have a genuine use, and are designed to raise the vibration by engaging different centers in conflict, thus creating positive and negative sides of a vibration frequency. It is said that one must have both angel and devil in continual warfare in order to succeed in the Work. This simply means that both positive and negative factors must be present in order to create a vibration. Vibrations do not occur with only one factor. That is why those who try to be "all good" or "only Essence" or "all sacrificing and no ordinary gratification" fail in their work. It takes both sides. One must have both psyche *and* Essence — conforming and nonconforming. No sugar without salt.

YOUR RELATIONSHIP, YOUR MIRROR $7.95

Why are you attracted to certain people? Secret knowledge about cycles that could make or break your relationship. Use your intimate relationship to radically improve your entire life. Attract your ideal consort (soul mate). Enjoy ecstasy with intimacy as you celebrate true romance. 90 minutes.

THE TANTRIC SECRET OF SEXUAL SATISFACTION $7.95

The secret skill, rarely mentioned in sex manuals, that makes any man or woman an incredible lover. This is the core talent, easily developed with practice, that is the key to total sexual satisfaction and subtle energy Tantric bliss. 60 minutes.

ZEN SEX cassettes are sold only as a set for $15.00.

ZEN SEX I. The Zen of Sex

Beyond goals to the sensory moment. How to experience sex exactly as it is without thinking or interpretation. Judeo-Christian upbringing and negative emotions. Bliss-tranquillity meditation, insight meditation and sex. Going beyond mind and ego. The bodymind is wave-like vibration. Through the void. Letting go of the bodymind. Beyond separation and unity to Cosmic playfulness and the perception of Reality. 90 minutes.

ZEN SEX II. Zen Sex in Practice

Special "Just Touch" technique for liberating the mind during lovemaking. Dare to relax. Breathing. Effects of positions. Dealing with unruly mental states. Affirmations and koans. Why long-term relationships lose their pizzazz. Sexual ritual. The inner game of romance and sexual fulfillment. The emotion of love vs. unconditional compassion and kindness. Using orgasm to open bodymind. Beyond man and woman. Tantric Orgasm. 90 minutes.

Audio cassettes are by David Alan Ramsdale unless otherwise noted. All cassettes are recorded in Dolby®.

ASTROLOGICAL CONSULTATIONS

David Alan Ramsdale is a professional astrologer in the areas of relationship, newborn/child and psychospiritual astrology. Candid yet deeply caring, he strives to uncover the very essence of your chart, revealing untapped talents and hidden strengths as well as blind spots and inner blocks. He is also a psychic and Tarot card reader.

In-depth astrological reading is $75. Chart comparisons are $50. Please include name, place, date and time (include a.m. or p.m.) of birth, sex, some background data (career, education, etc.) for each chart along with any questions you may have. For newborns and children, please include information about the parents. You will receive an attractive chart calculated with computer accuracy and a personalized 90 minute cassette interpretation. Payable to David A. Ramsdale, Astrology Dept., Peak Skill Publishing.

TANTRIC RELATIONSHIP CONSULTATIONS

David and Ellen, the co-authors of **Sexual Energy Ecstasy,** are available for consultations, presentations and seminars on Tantric lovemaking and Tantric marriage. Please contact them c/o Peak Skill Publishing.

PEAK SKILL PUBLISHING
P.O. BOX 5489
PLAYA DEL REY, CA 90296-5489

PEAK SKILL

Tantric Sex	$ 9.95	_____
Sexual Energy Ecstasy	$ 9.95	_____
Journey Through the Great Mother	$ 9.95	_____
Tantra - Bliss of Reality	$ 7.95	_____
Working with Sex Energy	$ 7.95	_____
Your Relationship, Your Mirror	$ 7.95	_____
Secret of Sexual Satisfaction	$ 7.95	_____
Zen Sex I & II	$15.00	_____

TOTAL FOR ITEMS IN THIS ORDER _____

CA RESIDENTS ADD 6% SALES TAX _____

SUBTOTAL _____

SHIPPING CHARGE $2.00

ORDER TOTAL _____

Our Unconditional Money-back Guarantee

If you are not satisfied with any book or tape you may return the undamaged item within 10 days for a complete refund of the purchase price.

Name: _____ _____

Address: _____ Apt. # _____

_____ ZIP: _____

CANADIAN/FOREIGN: U.S. funds only. Shipping charge is $4.00.